Torch and the Spear

Patrick Regan

CAPALL BANN PUBLISHING

Torch and the Spear

©1996 Patrick Regan

ISBN 1 898307 72 5

Cover design & illustration by Daryth Bastin

Published by:

Capall Bann Publishing
Freshfields
Chieveley
Berks
RG20 8TF

Children of the Night

by Patrick Regan

The Oak leaves catch gently the hot afternoon breeze,
They speak in a strange language lost to all but the chosen few.
Many once understood their incessant natural chatter
now lost in the midst of long long ago.
Night falls slowly, the solar orb has gone down deep
hissing into the grey blue sea.
The children of the night awaken.
From the clump of Scots Pines and old Owl voices concern,
" *Whoo Whoo* ", the voice of the night chorus jars intimate,
penetrating diamond hard knowing
into the mind of the quiet man under the moon stone.
With arms held high in well practiced grace
the man becomes one with himself and the place.
How many before him, how many to come
will hear the night children and follow their call?
Magickal light befriends long Moon shadows
into the silver circle through the tall dark trees.
The animal fear of not knowing, understanding, rationalising,
  evaluating,
the fear of leaving the clear light, logical world behind matters not at
  all now.
The lunar knowing, feeling, experiencing, is all important
and all that exists in this sacred ephemeral moment in time,
when the realms of the Gods conjoin with man's journey into self.

The last of the candles extinguished carries off into the astral sphere
the holy works performed earlier.
The night's deed is done and the solitary figure
leaves the ancient circle once again in darkness
to the lonely calls of the children of the night .

' Open Up '

Away from the crowd thought becomes clear,
  mundane and astral grow nearer and near.
Away from the crowd patently still,
  green becomes greener healing the ill.
Lightness and knowing illuminate the path,
darkness is conquered with powerful wrath.
Why is such magic not known to all?
Why is the like marked with a fall?
Those that disclose Autumn's first leaf, are treated with
  contempt just like the thief.
Those that bring knowledge shining so bright, are treated
  like villains and ejected with might
Ears do not harken, eyes do not see,
  the tiger that lurks down by the sea .
Soon it's too late Summer has gone,
  along with the Swallow, along with the Swan.
Winter draws near handle with care,
  the truth sometimes hurts, but don't blame the Bear.
Just open your eyes then you will see,
  the beauty of wisdom is yours and it's free .

The Torch and the Spear

Our ancient pre-Christian ancestors may not have possessed modern man's technology, expertise, social graces, communication abilities or capacity to travel at great speeds, but he/she made up for this by possessing something far more important. The andeluvial Pagan held a wisdom and understanding of Mother Earths natural cycles and moods, that modern man can only just sense as a distant psychic memory.

Our forefathers saw themselves as being part of the natural cosmic order of world events, not like contemporary man with his monotheistic patriarchal attitude of being above nature and the animal kingdom. This long forgotten wisdom was once sensed and known instinctively, not measured as something on a screen, monitor or computer in a laboratory.

Such wisdom is still here to be explored, and one of the most accessible paths to this goal is through the understanding of ancient myth and legend. This work will hopefully help the serious seekers discover the ancient latent truths that exist within, without and through ones-self, by interpretation of often unexplained or misunderstood mythological events.

At face value many legends seem like just nice entertaining stories told by Druids, Tribal Shamans, cunning wise folk and families of old. Many tales obviously helped a Saxon, Norse or Celtic clan get through an icy cold Winter's night, whilst huddled together around the embers of a blazing hearth fire. Stories of great battles, heroic deeds and lusty romances between Gods/Goddesses, Heroes/Heroines would have indeed stirred the blood of warrior and maiden alike.

On a deeper spiritual level, the same stories would carry on cultural traditional thought patterns and psychic home truths not at first apparent to a shallow thinking individual. Early man was no ignorant savage as modern Christian theologians would have us believe. He had to do one thing - survive, this meant knowing how he and the universal forces reacted with each other. Unlike modern man with his clocks, dates and calenders he followed the moods and changes of the seasons by looking and listening to the birds, fish, trees and weather. These things could not be ignored because his very survival depended on them - for if he followed the tracks of a bear or wolf accidentally instead of a stag, he could end up being a hot lunch. His senses were honed sharp like those of an animal, and he felt with his visceral powers correctly when something was right or wrong, because if he ever did get it wrong then there probably wouldn't be another chance.

This ancient knowledge became the stuff of myth and legend, passed from father to son by word of mouth or pattern on the cave wall. With the right mind-set it is possible to know what the myths of native tradition really meant and how they came to originate in the first place.

Our early Pagan ancestors must have realised the value of personifying the seasonal forces - Spring, Summer, Autumn and Winter, as a powerful way to bring elemental energy into an understandable focus. Mythological tales would have been an excellent way to warn one's offspring of the impending dangers of the harsh Winter to come, as a method of imparting knowledge into deeper sub conscious it was (and of course still is) unsurpassable, although many people may not realise this fact immediately.

4

The predecessors of these Isles were polytheistic in their religious concepts of life. Every stone, tree, river and season had it's allotted deity.

The often dramatic changes in natural seasonal cycles were frequently represented in terms of great battles between Gods and Goddesses. The evaluation that follows will illustrate this fact.

In one British legend 'Gwyn ap Nudd' (son of Nudd) is seen to do fierce battle for the hand of the beautiful maiden Creudylad, his opponent is the God 'Gwyrthur ap Greidawl'. This duel was to occur at every Feast of Beltaine on Mayday (the start of the Celtic Summer) until the end of time. Gwyn will be discussed in more detail later in the book, however it is sufficient here to explain him as a deity associated with death and the Celtic under-world. Conversely Gwyrthur his adversary, is viewed in this tale as being a God of a solar nature. Incidentally Gwyn's father Nudd/Lludd was not given the same amount of devotion and prominence as his son by later mythological writers. This is probably because Gwyn ap Nudd was to later absorb many stories through Norman/French Christian romancers, connected with the hugely popular legend of King Arthur and his Knights. Again, these deities will be examined in greater detail further on in the book. They are included here as mere examples in this hypothesis.

In the Welsh tale of Olwen (daughter of Yspaddaden the giant) and Culhwch, we see Culhwch having to win the giant's fair daughter from him by completing a number of impossible tasks, which eventually leads to the demise of Yspaddaden. Olwen is described in Welsh myth as being of intense beauty, she had hair so yellow that it made the Broom flowers of Spring pale by comparison. Wherever she stepped four white trefoil flowers would suddenly burst forth, which led to her name - Olwen meaning 'she of the white *track'*. This strangely beautiful reference of a maiden in who's trail follows wild flowers, gives us a clue to Olwen's true ancient identity; she is none other than the Goddess of Spring breathing her life-giving energy into the lovely blooms of May.

Accompanied by a party of knights Culhwch/Kulhwch (pronounced Keelhookh) the hero of this tale, approaches Olwen's father - *'Hawthorn chief of Giants'* (in Welsh - Yspaddaden Penkawr) to seek his permission to marry the fair maiden. The giant refused telling Culhwch to return again the next day, which he did with his entourage of King Arthur's finest warriors including Kai, Bedwyr, Kynddelig, Gwrhyr, Gwalchmei and Menw. With Culhwch this band of heroes seems to become a type of ancient *'Magnificent Seven'*. Hawthorn knew that losing his beautiful daughter would surely lead to his own death, so he plays for time by again and again insisting that Culhwch and his men return.

Hawthorn makes many excuses to keep his daughter from marriage, moreover in his grumpy outbursts he engages in a series of dangerous poison dart throwing contests, which finally leads to the giant being pierced through the eyeball by a well aimed attack from Culhwch himself. However, Hawthorn was not killed by this seemingly deadly blow, (which is very interesting as the Gaelic version of this myth, involving the God Lugh and his Fomorian adversary - Balor ends with Lugh killing the older God by a missile hitting him in his death-dealing eye). He merely curses and generally grumbles at Culhwch through his obvious pain and discomfort. Hawthorn tells the young suitor that his head burns, eyes water, and that he will curse the forge that created the infernal dart. Like the Gaelic God Lugh, Culhwch is represented here in this legend with solar attributes, one only has to stare into the hot Summer's Sun for a few seconds to appreciate the discomfort suffered by Hawthorn - soon one's eyes will sting and water if the gaze be- comes too long.

6

Hawthorn may not have been killed, however he had been severely disabled and humbled by his engagement in arms with Culhwch. By now the boot was on the other foot, the young suitor warned Hawthorn not to try his luck at further bouts of dart throwing and to this request the giant agreed. Culhwch and Hawthorn then sat opposite each other to discuss the price to be set for Olwen's hand in wed-lock by her malicious old father. The conversation gradually gained increasing momentum as Hawthorn told Culhwch of the enormous bride-price he demanded for Olwen.

Obviously Hawthorn had hoped to delay his own death further by setting such a high, seemingly impossible set of tasks for the young warrior to complete. The terms of the consent were as follows; firstly Culhwch had to provide food and drink for the wedding by cultivating and harvesting a large hill in only one day. This was a task deemed to be possible for none other than Amaethon son of Don, the God of Agriculture and Govannan the Smith God, these deities must also in turn have the assistance of six magic oxen.

Hawthorn had in his youth sowed nine bushels of flax which had never germinated, this next task implored Culhwch to actually gather this flax, for use in making the white wimple (head clothing) for Olwen's fair head. He must also gain honey far sweeter than even the best untouched swarm could create, in fact it had to be nine times sweeter than any other to touch the lips of man or Gods, this was needed to furnish mead for the wedding party.

Next Hawthorn demanded thirteen treasures to be granted to him as a dowry for Olwen;

> To hold the sweet honey the magic vessel of Llwyr son of Llwyryon.

The basket of Gwyddneu Garanhir was needed to hold all of the food for the wedding, the basket could hold enough food to feed every person in the world many times over.

The cauldron of the Gael-Giwrnach to prepare the wedding feast.

The magical horn to drink out of, that belonged to Gwlgawd Gododin.

The mystical harp of Teirtu which could play by itself without the help of human hand.

The white tusk of the King of Boars that had to be extracted from the beast while it was still alive had to be gained to cut the hair of Hawthorn.

Hawthorn's hair had to be made soft with the blood of the perfectly black sorceress, daug.

The perfectly white sorceress from the source of the Stream of Sorrow on the boundaries of Annwn (the other world).

The bottles of Gwyddolwyn Gorr that kept any fluid warm, were to be also taken in order to prevent the black sorceress's blood from becoming chilled.

The bottles of Rhinnon Rhin Barnawd were needed for the wedding guests milk, these magic vessels ensured that any milk would never ever become soured

Next the sword of Gwrnach the giant.

Lastly the comb, razor and scissors of Twrch Trwyth, the King who could transform himself into the awesome shape of a fearsome wild boar.

It is of course obvious that Culhwch was of a divine nature, he had to be in order to complete these massive tasks. Legend tells us that he virtually laughs in the face of such seemingly impossible deeds, and is not daunted in any way whatsoever. The Arthurian Knights that accompany Culhwch in this quest are also much more than merely brave heroes, they display here all the divine attributes and abilities that connect them to the earlier Celtic deities on which they are based. Menus, for instance, could achieve invisibility at will for both himself and his comrades at arms. While Gwrhyr possessed the enviable ability to be able to understand the languages of all men, trees, birds and animals.

Culhwch owed much to his valiant company of assistants, together they helped him complete the incredible quest set before him by Hawthorn the giant. On seeing all the wondrous treasures laid out before him by Culhwch, Hawthorn finally admitted defeat. Following this victory the giant was killed by Goreu son of Custennin, and his head impaled upon a tall pole for all his many enemies to see. Olwen was now free to marry Culhwch, which she did with due haste the very same night.

The Arthurian story of Tristrem/Tristan and Ysolt (also known as Iseult/Ysonde) is a story of great tragedy and romance. Originally this particular romance was unconnected with the Round Table cycle of events. However as with a multitude of other old Pagan tales, it gradually seeped through into the very fabric of later Christianisations of Arthurian legend. Tristrem was the love child of King Mark of Cornwall's sister and Roland of Ermonie.

THE WHITE SAIL
PUR.

During his 15th year Tristrem went to Cornwall where he became extremely popular with all the folk at court, wooing many with his charming minstrel skills. He did battle with Moraunt and succeeded in killing him, however Tristrem himself was badly wounded which was to lead to him recuperating for three years in Ireland. This was the land where he met Ysolt - daughter of the Queen, who treated him kindly and made him whole again.

On his return to Cornwall Tristrem told his uncle all about the marvellous Irish princess and her wondrous beauty. Mark was highly impressed by Tristrem's tale of Ysolt, so he commanded him to escort her back to England in the hope of marrying her. Life and love are as we know never that simple, and King Mark's affections were no exception, for Tristrem and Ysolt both unwittingly drank a magic love potion which was strictly intended for Mark's lips only. From that day on till their deaths, not one single man could ever come between their true love for each other. Ysolt reluctantly married King Mark, however she with the assistance of her trusty maid Brengwain, continued to meet Tristrem secretly. Later, Tristrem was exiled from Cornwall, however fate had it that he was to again come back to the Cornish land, where his affair with Ysolt was to begin anew.

Tristrem visited many lands, including Brittany, Spain and Ermonie. He married another lady who was surprisingly also called by the same name as his true love. He was badly wounded in combat and his thoughts again turned to his only love; Ysolt of Ireland. A messenger was thereby sent to fetch his lover to him, Tristrem told the messenger to put up a *'white sail'* if she has returned with him, alternatively if Ysolt is not on board then let the sail be *'black'*. Ysolt of Ireland, eager to again be with her lover joined the messenger and sets sail.

'BLODEUWEDD'

P.V.R.

As soon as the ship was sighted Tristrem rises from his sick bed and anxiously asks what colour sail does she carry? Of course the sail is white, however Tristrem's wife filled with envy and hatred for her husband's lover, tells Tristrem that the sail is black. This is more than the heart-sick man can bear, he cannot face life any longer without his true love so he sinks back into his bed and tearfully dies. Ysolt of Ireland arrived, and on finding out what has happened she subsequently dies of a broken heart on the bosom of her stricken Tristrem.

King Mark was informed as to the circumstances surrounding the lovers demise, he cannot have been a jealous man for he buried them both in the same grave. They planted a rose bush and vine over this place, legend has it that they grew so tightly intertwined that no man could from that day on, ever separate them.

This most beautiful of Celtic romances was so understandably popular that it's telling spread far from it's origins, and similar tales are common throughout Europe. The Celtic people were often only credited with cunning and ferocity, however this particular story gives us a deep insight into the great Celtic love of poetry, art and romance.

Another myth finds the flower-bride Blodeuwedd, wife of the Welsh God Llew plot Llew's death with her lover Gronw Pebr God of night. The Welsh God of Magic ' *Math* ' and *'Gwydion'* son of Don who was Llew's father, joined forces to create a wife for Llew. They gathered the blossoms of Broom and Meadowsweet, mixed them with Oak and together produced the most beautiful of maidens ever seen by man or Gods. Because of the maid's stunning beauty they decided to name her *'Blodeuwedd'* which means *'flower face'*. Blodeuwedd and Llew were then given a great palace to reign over which was called Mur-y-castell, nearby to Bala Lake in Wales.

'THE WISE ONE'

For one season life seemed tranquil and idyllic for the happy couple, until one particular day a huntsman came by the palace, and slew a stag at nightfall. Blodeuwedd found herself strangely fascinated by this handsome rider who introduced himself as Gronw Pebyr (one of the Gods of darkness and Winter). Llew was at that time away visiting Math, so Blodeuwedd invited the stranger to join her in the palace for food and drink. That night the two fell deeply in love and the smitten flower-bride plotted with Gronw Pebyr, as to how best they could rid themselves of poor Llew.

When Llew returned Blodeuwedd cleverly tricked him into revealing his secret of how his life might be taken. Llew innocently told his devious wife that he could not be killed inside or outside of a house, he could not be killed on horseback or on foot. However he could be slain by a lance that had taken a whole year to craft, it must have been only worked upon on the day of the Sunday sacrifice. This weapon had to be thrown at Llew when he was under a thatched roof, had just bathed, with one foot on the bath's edge the other placed upon a male goat's back. If these requirements were made then he would surely die. Gronw quickly began to do work on the lance, and in one year it was ready to use against Llew. Gronw told Blodeuwedd when he had finished the weapon, so with haste she again tricked Llew into actually showing her how he might be killed.

Trusting his devious wife, Llew agreed to her strange request. So under a thatched roof she made ready the bath for him and tied a goat by it, Llew proceeded to enjoy this ablution, however Blodeuwedd had also given Gronw instructions to meet at this place, After his bath, Llew in getting out of his bathing cauldron placed one foot on the edge and the other upon the tethered billy goat's back. Without hesitation Gronw hurled the lance from his ambush position, thereby it struck Llew. The shaft broke and with a pitiful scream he transformed into an Eagle and flew away.

PVR. 95.

' THE WHITE GODDESS:

Llew never returned and Gronw gained all of his estate and added it to his own, together with the hand of Blodeuwedd. Wondering where his son had disappeared to, Gwydion set out to search in every place for him. While in North Wales, Gwydion came upon a lonely man who complained grievously about his old sow. The animal he discovered would disappear all day only to return at night, this affair fascinated Gwydion so he proceeded to follow the sow. She ventured far and wide until she came to a brook between Snowdon and the shore which is now called *'Nat-y-Llew'* and stopped there, feeding under an Oak tree on lumps of rotten meat. Gwydion looked up and was surprised to see an Eagle shaking off pieces of putrid meat. Without doubt this must be Llew he thought, and thereby proceeded to sing a magical verse to the Eagle. Gradually the nervous bird began to descend a little at a time down the old Oak tree until, after Gwydion fully gained it's trust, the Eagle reached his lap. He tapped the bird with his magical staff and Llew returned to his original form.

Llew was a terrible sight, his muscles wasted, bones prominent and skin torn like paper, but time passed by and he was fully healed. The father and son journeyed back to the palace, where they executed vengeance on their devious foes. Llew killed the God Gronw with a spear that pierced a large rock before finding it's target.

Blodeuwedd was cast into darkness and ironically turned into an owl (another bird of prey no less, yet of night instead of day). Finally Llew re-took possession of his estate and reigned forever more in great prosperity.

This particular story of a disloyal bride is quite likely to have been incorporated into later Christianised Norman romances, such as King Arthurs rivalry with Lancelot over their love for Queen Guinevere. Without doubt many great myths and legends such as the above do indeed have their origins in true tales of human relationships however their real lasting power comes to us as something much deeper than mere man-made poetic romance.

Take for instance the God Gwynn ap Nudd and his battle with Gwythyur for Creudylad. Gwynn is here in this particular myth taking on the guise of the cold dark half of the Celtic year which is of course Winter. Gwythyur is the light half - the season of Summer. Their perpetual battle is the eternal struggle for Spring's fleeting green months represented as Creudylad.

The battle betwixt Winter and Summer continues in the tales of Tristrem and Ysolt Olwen and Culwch and Llew and Blodeuwedd. References to Olwen as 'she of the white track' and Blodeuwedd as 'flower face' prove without doubt that all such maidens represent the fleeting energy force inherent in Spring and early Summer. The Hawthorn or Quickthorn Tree (crataegus monogyna) gives us the name of Hawthorn the Giant father of Olwen. He was indeed a thorny old creature however we must remember that the Hawthorn is often in mythology referred to as the Goddess tree or tree of the white Goddess.

This of course furthers the hypothesis of flower maids and brides being, in fact, remnants of the great Earth Mother herself albeit in the aspect of young virgin of Spring. Ysolt again becomes the ephemeral beauty fought over by two rivals (Winter and Summer) - King Mark and Tristrem. As we know, both Ysolt and Tristrem (as Spring and Summer) die together leaving the land barren for Winter's (Mark's) reign. In the tale of the light God Llew and his unfaithful bride we observe a type of analogy that tells a similar but opposite story.

Here the battle between Winter and Summer is often represented as two opposing armies fighting for a land or Kingdom. Like most conquering races, the Gaelic Celts attacked the indigenous peoples of Ireland not only with sword, sling-shot and spear. but by reducing and vilifying their religious belief systems.

The native folk of the land became the Fomorians (undersea giants) and as such the Celtic invaders made sure that every possible association with death, slaughter and evil was laid upon them. There is doubtless much confusion as to whether or not, the Fomorians were an actual race of men or primitive deities. In all probability they were both the aboriginal people and also the mysterious Gods and Goddesses handed down to us now as grotesque Fomorian Giants.

The first Celtic immigrants would have started to amalgamate with the native people, much as Saxon, Norse and Teuton did in Britain. Sooner or later certain original sacred sites evolved. Myths and deities must have impressed the Gaels enough to make them want to incorporate them into their own credos. Similar affairs happened following the Roman Conquest of Britain, with several deities impressing the legions so much that they felt compelled to embrace them.

The Celtic horse Goddess Epona (who gives us the word Pony) was one such adoption. During early fierce pitched battles the Roman troops were highly surprised to learn how dangerously skillful the Celtic charioteers really were. These proud horsemen would check their steeds at full speed on a steep incline, then instantly turn them, run along the pole, stand on the yoke, then get back into their chariots without wasting any time at all.

On hearing of the Celtic Goddess Epona, naturally the Roman cavalry units would have taken no chances in missing the first opportunity to fully link with this obviously effective Goddess form - why take risks when the answer was crystal

pva.

DANA.

20

clear? They would later of course have much greater reason to fear Epona's warriors when the Icenian Queen Boadicea/Boadicca led a crushing revolt at Colchester and London in 60AD. Epona seems to be responsible for the taboo against eating horse meat, a strong abhorrence that still remains deep in British consciousness.

The famous tale of Lady Godiva who in 1041 rode naked through Coventry in an attempt to persuade her husband Earl Leofric of Mercia to reduce oppressive town taxes, seems to have assimilated several aspects of the Epona myth. It is quite sad to see such a proud and once sacred beast like the horse, now reduced to a form of mere entertainment at the local race track, *'a means to just winning a few quid'* on a Saturday afternoon. Thanks for this state of affairs rests with the advancement of technology and birth of the modern *'horse-less'* carriage. Progress? I wonder.

The original inhabitants of Ireland, the Fomorians had many battles with various invaders of that Emerald Isle. The most famous being the Tuatha de Danaan (people of the Goddess Danu). The night of Samhain, (31st October) marks the start of the Celtic Winter and end of their Summer. It was on this hallowed eve that Gods and Giants with their awesome armed forces commenced battle. Naturally this titanic struggle reflected the warfare of the Gaelic people and their savage aboriginal opponents on a physical level. The fact that this combat started on the eve of Samhain, Summers end provides us with the vital clue as to it's long forgotten primitive meaning.

With it's severe hardships Winter was of course to be feared and respected. It was a time of suffering and death, a period in the year's cycle when many young, old or infirm members of the tribe would succumb to illness, often indeed resulting in death. By associating the dread of Winter's chill with the evils of Fomorian attack, peoples like the Gaels gave fear and combat a special kind of dignity, making fear itself not something to hide from, but instead a force to be met head on and defeated with courage.

Such a profoundly philosophical outlook on the universal scale of life gives us deep insight into how our ancient forebears saw themselves.

The personification of a single deity as a seasonal force such as Winter or Summer is in effect the very same concept in a different guise as the representation of a race of Gods/Giants matching the very same elemental force. It would seem feasible that early man first portrayed the seasons as singular deities simply because early human society back in the Palaeo/Neo lithic eras were principally made up as small hunting gathering units. The concept of military offensive action between two or more conflicting armies had not yet then been fully developed. The second clue to lead us into a greater understanding of the light/Summer bringing pantheon like the Tuatha de Danaan is the legendary belief that they first set foot on Irish soil on Beltaine day, thus bringing in the Summer.

In like fashion the first Gaelic men arrived later, also on the day of Summer's initiation. These mythical Celtic stories would have been passed down from father to son over great periods in time. Frequently containing unadulterated truths and wisdom gleaned from the Celts own Stone-Age ancestors. The earliest pastoralists and farmers, the neolithic people, worshipped the great Goddess, the Earth Mother.

Many of her original titles have disappeared in the mists of time, however we can rely on myths and legends of races like the Celt, Saxon or Norse to provide us with knowledge of man's age-old desire to magically connect with the cosmic currents of the universe. The majority of ancient cultures regarded the principle of divinity as being first feminine, a

Mother Goddess. Gods showed up later in man's evolutionary development.

During the final part of the last Glaciation the Magdalenian peoples of France and Western Europe began to produce many fine examples of bone spears, needles, necklaces and most interestingly to us, Mother Earth type Goddess figurines. Rudimentary human understanding of the sexual process was probably limited, resulting in the concept of divine - virginal birth! Women gave birth annually just like the great Goddess of the Earth herself, bringing forth the green flows of Summer's joy. The later inevitable realisation that the male was vital to fertility resulted in the incorporation of Gods, and the essential balanced view of divinity then began to evolve.

To the people of the Neolithic era the very landscape itself was a reflection of the great Goddess, her feast days being celebrated throughout the year at numerous megaliths, circles, and hill-top sites. Two well known mountains found in the vicinity of Killarney (Ireland) give evidence to the Earth Mother's hold over human consciousness 'The Paps of Ana'. Ana or Anu is merely another title for the Celtic Danu herself. At Avebury, Wiltshire the collection of neolithic circles and long barrows are arranged to form the massive outline of the Goddess into the living landscape. She was sensed by early man in the opening buds, thawing ice and lighter days of Spring. Man knew that it was essential to relate intimately with nature in order to know himself and the divinity that worked through him.

The Celtic Goddess Brigit or Bride, was associated with the coming Spring and the start of the lambing season. An old Celtic Folktale tells of Brigit annually liberating the Earth from the grip of the blue-faced hag of Winter, the Cailleach Bheur. In the Isle of Man the hag was known as the Caillagh ny Groamagh meaning the old gloomy woman. The hag is

BRigiT.   PVR.

sometimes portrayed as a giant bird, and it is interesting to note that the Gaelic war Goddess the Morrigu/Morrigan often takes the guise of a black crow. Believing in the power of transformation - shapeshifting, it is easy to see why the Celts associated carrion scavengers like the crow with war, death and untimely Winter's power. Crows and other meat-eating birds would have been very common visitors to the sites of battle-fields, so accordingly they were linked with the dark hag of Winter, the Morrigan.

In Britain the dark cold lady took on the name of Black-Annis and it is probable that this name connects with the Gaelic Ana/ Anu. Another aspect of the Morrigan is Badb - the fury who was believed to move over (like a crow) battle-fields inspiring Celtic warriors to heroic deeds. Later the dark sinister side of the old lady takes on the guise of the Banshee, who's morbid wailing forewarns of impending doom and disaster. Each Gaelic clan worth it's salt had it's own exclusive Banshee. The Banshee legend may hark back to the story of the hero Cuchulainn who was confronted by three hags (the dark Goddess in her triple aspect) before his last conflict. They shamed him into eating the flesh of a hound, a food that was taboo to him, this caused the hero to be left half paralysed and later at his death a crow perched on his shoulder.

Cuchulainn's demise following his meeting with the battle Goddess, marks another theme in the mythological cycle, that is the battle between death and life. In many ways this hero, like his spiritual father Lugh, was associated with the victory of light over darkness, although in this particular legend Cuchulainn becomes the victim marking Winter's conquest over the light of Summer. He is also in this role of the 'tempted one' taking on the aspect of man's fear of his own subconscious dread of weakness and old age.

PVR.   THE MORRIGU.

The essential balance between Winter and Summer plays it's inevitable timeless tune in this rich tale. The dreaded wail of the Banshee links intimately with the fierce battle cry of the Gaelic supreme War Goddess the Morrigu, who inspired the brave into combat. It is necessary to imagine several things to appreciate how the battle cry of the Morrigu became embedded deep in Celtic consciousness. First one must try to mentally stand with the front line of a waiting Celtic war party, tensions would, of course, be very high as a hated enemy such as a Roman infantry unit appeared ready to engage you and your comrades.

The adrenaline pumps blood swiftly through the veins and arteries, swords rattle against shields, battle horns ring out to terrify the enemy and inspire valour in your troop. All these moments converge to produce a *'hum'* of battle. Finally your chieftain raises his blade - a signal to attack, which is followed by the menacing cry of charging warriors. These many images of the noise of battle became personified in the Celtic mind as the war cry of the Morrigu, whilst above raging fires and clashing weapons of engagement the raucous calls of the hoodie crow reminded brave men that the dark Goddess was close at hand, ready to claim her grisly toll.

The triple aspect of feminine divinity mentioned in the previous exploits of Cuchulainn and the three hags is common to many cultures through history. Very often they are portrayed as old crones possessing the inherent ability of divination. To the Norsemen they were the Norns - Goddesses of Fate called Verdandi, Skuld and Urd. From Urd we get the word - wurd meaning weird, she appeared very old and decrepit (the past), Verdandi was young and attractive (the present), whilst Skuld became associated with future events and was portrayed as closely veiled, not to be seen.

Personifications of past, present and future (the fates) have been passed down through to present day literature often, as

FULL MOON.
PVR 45.

personalities like the three weird sisters in Shakespeare's Macbeth, Godmother's in fairy stories, or even possibly Cinderella and the two ugly sisters. Originally the triple aspect of the great Goddess would have related to her in the role of the three phases of the lunar cycle i.e. waxing, full and waning, this in turn linked intimately to the menstrual (mene - means moon in old Greek) cycle in women.

Interestingly the women in ancient tribal society (and modern Moon Goddess worshippers) realised that by relating fully, by honouring the Goddess, to the monthly - moonthly tides they would in turn all reach the peak of menstrual flow during the moon's full period. Such powerful and obviously effective moon magic would now seem quite strange to modern Westernised women living a busy and stressful 9-5 lifestyle, however it gives us an insight into the ancient wisdom of our pre-Christian Pagan ancestors' way of life. The three aspects of the Goddess also correlate to the ages of women, Maiden (childhood - puberty), Mother (maturity) and Crone (wisdom and old age). The triad of Goddesses show up again in the Celtic tale of the Milesian march on Tara which was the capital of the Tuatha De Danann.

The Milesians were the ancestors of the Gaels, and on arriving in Ireland they were approached by three Goddesses - the first, Banba told their Druid Amergin that the Milesian cause was not just, she then asked him to name the land after her - he agreed to this request. Further on the march they meet a second Goddess called Fotla who also asked for the land to be granted her title. Finally the Milesians met the third, Eriu who greeted them with good, kind words,

> *"To you that have come from afar this island shall henceforth belong, and from the setting to the rising sun there is no better land. And your race will be the most perfect the world has ever seen".*

The Druid Amergin then thanked Eriu for her prophecy, however Donn the son of Mile abruptly butted in telling Eriu that whatever blessings they had were only because of their own strengths. This angered the Goddess who told Donn that her prophecy didn't concern him, and that neither he nor his descendants would live long enough to enjoy the land. After this warning Eriu asked Amergin to name the land after her, just as the other Goddesses had done previously. The name Eriu in its' genetic form Erinn gives us now the modern day Ireland. This ancient tale leads us to the understanding of Celtic respect for native deities, many were of course to be twisted into monstrous creatures like the Fomorians of earlier legends. However some were incorporated into the Celts very ethos.

The three Goddesses Eriu, Fotla and Banba are portrayed here as deities of the land its-self, a type of Genius Loci protecting Ireland from invasion. They are also like the Viking Norns' Goddesses of divination having the ability to prophecise. The Milesian invaders realised that it was wise to appease the local deities first, as Amergin's politeness to the Goddesses proved.

Their names as in Eriu (leading to Ireland) bear witness to the powerful effect they must have had on Celtic consciousness. Eriu's prophecy regarding Donn was soon to become fatally true when he lost his life by drowning in the sea. Here we see, once again, shades of the dark Goddess, ever ready to prognosticate the doom of those nearing the end of their earthly quest. Eriu was herself of the Tuatha De Danann, however she begat a child called Bress with Elatha/Elathan who was a Fomorian.

The handsome Bress and Elathan became the personification of man's dark sinister side, the very part of themselves that had to be Eriu's prophecy regarding Donn was soon to become fatally true when he lost his life by drowning in the sea. Here we see once again shades of the dark Goddess, ever ready to prognosticate the doom of those nearing the end of their earthly quest. Eriu was herself of the Tuatha De Danann, however she begot a child called Bress with Elatha/Elathan who was a Fomorian.

There are numerous examples in Celtic mythology regarding marriage and partnerships between people of the Goddess Danu and the Fomorians. This is obviously displaying on a physical level the ancient folk memory of actual historical integration between the new Celtic race and the Aboriginal stock of the land. On the deeper spiritual level, these often stormy relationships relate to the land, sea elements and most of all, as previously mentioned, the eternal battle between Summer and Winter.

The Fomorians were not by any means always portrayed as ugly Giants with grotesque features. Elathan was described as *"a man of fairest form"*, with long golden hair he wore fine clothes and jewellery inlaid with precious stones and gold. His son Bress was also extremely handsome - Bress meaning beautiful. Here we see an interesting twist in mythological thought patterns, Fomorians like Bress and his father Elathan have here taken on the role of dark, clever Princes/Kings, handsome but not to be trusted.

The Celts prove in this context that they were very well aware of *'All that glitters is not gold'*, this shows us that Celtic intellectualism was then at a very sophisticated level, and not as was often thought, the barbaric mentality of misunderstood ancient races. The Celtic people realised that danger came in many forms and not only was it to be seen as monstrous or ugly. The handsome Bress and Elathan became the personification of man's dark sinister side, the very part of themselves that had to be faced without fear because fear itself was to the Gaelic warrior something to be conquered and defeated. The Fomorians were associated with the deep

JuNo·

PVR.95

sea, the sea itself was a place of danger and death, a fear to be overcome.

The Pagan Celts unlike their later Christian successors realised that their personification of the universal dark forces (i.e. the Fomorians) in nature were not in themselves evil. The Fomorians were necessary to keep a healthy balance in the general run of things, one couldn't have dark without light, nor have summer without winter. This vital equilibrium in nature was personified in several ways, most clearly by the concept of *'divine marriage'*. Bress the Fomorian dark one is married to Brigit of the light sided Tuatha De Danann. At the same time Cian of the Tuatha-De is wed to Ethniu, daughter of the Fomor Balor. The cosmic unchanging pattern of natural death and rebirth was set in Celtic legend for eternity. Reincarnation was part of Celtic belief, they understood that man would eventually leave his earthly existence, however he would also be one day born again into yet another incarnation, to continue his journey into spiritual enlightenment.

The belief in reincarnation inspired the Celtic warrior to commit brave deeds, for death was regarded as being not an end but a new beginning. Very often the Celts would fight naked except for neck torc, belt and helm, with their hair combed into fearsome spikey ruffs. They were renowned for their sheer arrogance, defiant resolve and bravado, giving enemies such as the Roman legions grave cause for alarm. Plain examples of this fact include the Icenian Queen Boadicea's revolt on London in 60 AD, and the possible Brigantian destruction of the Roman 9th legion at York (Eboracum) in 120 AD.

It has to be added here that some doubt remains over what actually happened to the mysterious 9th legion. Some authorities believe that this unit was withdrawn from Britain   (in 108-122 AD), only to meet their doom in Judaea

MINERVA.

P.V.R. 95.

around 132-135 AD, more evidence is needed to clarify this issue.

The Celtic tribe of the Brigantes that ruled a vast area in Northern Britain gets it's name from the Goddess Brigantia, who equates with the Gaelic Brigit - Goddess of fire, poetry and the hearth. In Eastern France she was known as Brigindo, moreover the Romans equated her with their Goddess Minerva.

Incidentally Minerva's name was thought to spring from the same root as 'mens' (mind). The ancient Latin scholar and critic 'Varro' believed her to be an impersonation of divine thought. In the materialistic plan of universal events, the great God Jupiter presided as Creator while Juno was seen as the representative.

These two deities reigned supremely over human destiny and evolution on manifold levels. However it was Minerva who overlooked divine intentions, will and ideas. Her festival took place between the 19th to 23rd March inclusive. Minerva was also equated with the native Celtic Goddess 'Sulis', who was worshipped at Bath which the Romans called 'Aquae Sulis' or 'Aquae Solis'.

Bath's thermal springs with their famous curative powers have been known for centuries. Bath was founded before Roman interruption in 863BC by Prince Bladud. The temple of 'Sulis' was believed to have been built when Bladud, who was afflicted by a nasty skin disorder, used the hot mud at the spring to heal himself, soon after he founded the Goddesses sacred temple at this location. The term 'mineral water' may possibly have a connection with Minerva (Minerva's water), who of course was widely revered at the same place.

NEPTUNE
PUR.

Modern Pagans could not do better than visit this ancient place, sacred to Minerva/Sulis when in need of a spiritual uplift, moreover Bath's deities provide ample evidence of Roman religious tolerance.

Contrary to popular belief the Roman state was in the wider sense, not suppressive of foreign religious beliefs, many deities like Sulis, Lludd or Brigit were merely equated and incorporated into their own religious mythos. Only Judaism and Christianity were deemed to be threatening to the empire and state security, because of their exclusively absolutist nature, and demand for total intolerant allegiance against other more tolerant Pagan faiths.

Roman influence radically changed the Celtic religion, deities that were previously conceived in an abstract form, would now often be skillfully portrayed by craftsmen in an increasingly human form. Examples of this type of Roman Celtic work can be found throughout Britain and Europe. Divinity had been advanced into a new iconographic era, deities that represented every conceivable aspect of human life-cycle and nature flourished.

In Britain and Ireland virtually every watercourse had it's own respective God or Goddess. Coventina was a popular water Goddess worshipped at Carrawburgh, Northumberland; she was often represented as a divine trinity which gives evidence to her importance. Vast amounts of coinage and bronze offerings were recovered from her sacred shrine near Hadrian's Wall, this was a common occurrence at many holy wells, springs and river temples. The River Thames that winds through London gets it's name from the Goddess Tamesis; the River Boyne in Ireland is named after the Goddess Boann who is linked to the flood myth of Celtic creation legends.

Boann was the Dagda, (Celtic Earth God's) wife, and her curiosity drove her to approach a forbidden well (source of the River Boyne), this Forced the waters to overflow and never return, thus the River Boyne was created. It is interesting to note that the River Shannon was also believed to have burst forth from a sacred well in a similar fashion, after interlacing with the Goddess Sinann/Sionan.

The association of these and other native Goddesses connected with water, links inextricably with fertility, and this in turn with the moon.

The ancient peoples of these Isles realised instinctively that the Moon's pull influenced tidal action, and that like women, water gave birth to new life. The flood myths intimately connect with the menstrual flow on an unconscious level, to many Celtic minds this lunar-flow was of course feminine, so naturally water, moon and fertility (another aspect of divine trinity) converged in the Goddess as Celtic legends show.

On the day of Samhain (Oct. 31st - Nov. 1st) the Dagda, God of the Earth copulated with the Morrigu who as we know often took on a triple guise. This act of earthly fertilisation occurred with the Goddess straddling the river, a foot placed precariously on each bank. The Dagda had a wife with three names, (another triple aspect) - Breng (lie), Meng (guile) and Meabel (disgrace). This deity bore him three daughters all named Brigit, yet one more connection with the thesis in question.

The Celts, observing the moon rise apparently out of the earth, crossing the river, then sinking in the Western sky, obviously considered this to be a magical sacred event, that had to be portrayed in an understandable yet divinely respectful way. Thus the mysterious lunar phase became that of the Goddess, and woman-kind. Brigit was in her triple aspect a Goddess of poetry, healing and fertility, as a representation of fertility and healing she does indeed connect to the elemental nature of water, but what on her link to poetry? Nothing is ever that simple in Celtic myth and Brigit is no exception.

The British and Gaelic people were highly impressed with the gentle art of the poet and minstrel, indeed Brigit's father the Dagda possessed a magic harp called the Four Angled Music, which probably linked to his ability to control the four seasons. Poetry was regarded as a *'fire of the soul'* and music indeed had the magical power to sooth the wounded spirit, thus these talents must have been of a divine nature to our forefathers' way of thinking. The Celts most likely adopted many of the older religious practices of native megalithic races that would often include solar deities. Brigit herself has associations with both fire and water. In Britain her namesake Brigantia gives her title to the rivers Braint and Brent, and her associations with the therapeutic qualities of water are obvious to see.

Being a divine child of the Earth God, Brigit therefore takes on the role of fire and water. Early man may be responsible for this original train of thought, as both fire and water do indeed arise out of the good earth, like Brigit. She is also to be seen arising as fire like the sun, and like the moon which connects to the element of water.

Brigit is a very complete Goddess in many ways, and her attributes must surely link to man's earliest folk memories and feelings of connection with the very planet itself. The great Celtic Brigit was Christianised and turned into the Irish St Brigit or Bride who took on all the feast days, sacred sites, associations and attributes of the much beloved earlier Goddess. The early Christian theologians obviously deemed it wiser to adopt, not suppress worship of beloved Pagan deities in this way. Thereby winning over more converts to the new Eastern religion.

'BRIGANTIA'

P.V.R.

The Celtic Spring feast of Imbolg (meaning in the belly) was later Christianised as Candlemass (festival of lights), Brigit was associated with this festival that is held at the start of February. She hereby takes command of the season from the blue hag of Winter. Her return marks the beginning of the first glimmers of pale light and the start of Spring, a time when the first snowdrops push through Winter's frost, and lambs come bleating down the cold meadows.

Brigit in her native British form of Brigantia remains in contemporary consciousness as the Britannia sovereign deity of Britain found on pre-decimal coinage, and of course in songs like *'Rule Britannia'* (Britannia rules the waves).

Again the waves concept harks back to the element of water. Young people inspired to nationalistic pride at the *'Proms'* concerts whilst chanting this song will probably be wholly unaware of the vast Pagan heritage that went to create their joyous sense of patriotism, and the link remaining to Brigantia, Goddess of their own Celtic ancestors.

The Britannia figure depicted on old coinage is resplendent with helmet, trident and shield, and one may wonder what this has to do with a Celtic Goddess associated with Spring and fertility. The answer lies with the Roman's indirect equation of Brigantia with their Goddess Minerva, who was patroness of soldiers, scholars and artisans. Britannia was originally struck on British coins by the Roman invaders to these Isles. Moreover, the use of the trident in the Britannia depiction, once again leads us into the element of water, as the trident itself was Neptune's (Roman Sea God) most well known attribute.

The three-pronged trident is again blatantly suggestive of the sacred trinity and all her many associations therein. Roman gladiatorial contests often featured a retiarius armed with a trident and net, two instruments intimately connected with water. These symbols of the marine realm bring us to realise that, they are as such powerfully symbolic of the waters of the deep unconscious mind, ultimately linking with the pure mystery of the Lunar cycle, evident in that magical card known to Tarot readers as the Moon.

The Celtic peoples held the powers of eloquence and poetry as ranking highly above mere sword play and aggression. As such we see here a primitive beginning leading up to the proverb *"the pen is mightier than the sword"*. Brigit as a Goddess of poetry here takes on the representation of fire - not in effect physical fire but intellectual or even spiritual fire, that lights the darkest recesses of a gravely troubled soul. The Christian St. Brigit's shrine at Kildare in Ireland contained a sacred fire, kept alight constantly by Nuns. In all probability this, like many other holy sites was originally used by Pagans as a place of worship.

During the feast of St Brigit, (Imbolg) at the beginning of February, people would construct small four-armed rushwork crosses then cast them alight - blazing into the night air. This rite was performed to hasten the coming of the Goddess and Spring growth. Incidentally, there used to be a similar ritual in Valdi Ledro (Tyrol), whereby a straw effigy of a woman was set alight, the figure interestingly was known as *'the old woman'*, this is without doubt a very ancient event. The old woman is the dark hag of Winter, by burning the effigy Spring was seen to be let in. Such rites originated many thousands of years ago, they enabled early man to intimately link with the cosmic forces that worked through and within him.

In Bavaria and it's neighbouring regions, folk would construct a large wheel of tarred straw, then from the top of a hill set it alight and watch it rush blazing down the slope. The rolling fire wheel may be seen as an original basis for that ancient solar symbol - the swastika, used throughout

42

history by various cultures including the Celts, Hindus, Germanic peoples and many others.

Neolithic man saw the sun itself travel, blazing across the noonday sky, it was a natural progression to represent this powerful image particularly at the festivals of solar reverence. The Celtic people unlike their predecessors were mainly cattle rearing folk, their four festivals - Imbolg, Beltaine, Lugnassad and Samhain were related to the two seasons, Summer and Winter, that Celtic culture recognised. However there is a strong probability that they did indeed adopt some earlier indigenous beliefs. Later Roman influence would most certainly have resulted in a strong cultural change in religious thinking.

The Romans, being agricultural people, venerated solar deities such as Mithras, and much confusion has resulted over the years as to whether sites like Stonehenge were used by Druidic priests for solar worship or not, the answer is yes and also no. Megalithic peoples who built the sacred Irish/British sites would certainly have worshipped sun deities as the life-giving energy Force of the cosmos. Then the invading Celts who at first being travelling people didn't have much use for solar divinities, would as we have seen above in some instances adopted the earlier deities of fire/sun. The arrival in Britain of Roman cultural influence and Eastern sun Gods made an irreversible impact on the Celts, who by now were becoming increasingly converted to being reliant on the sun and farming crops. Out of this maelstrom of religious and philosophical transformation arose many Romano-Celtic deity assimilations.

Mider - God of the Gaelic underworld was equated with the Roman Pluto. Mider was a son of the Earth God Dagda, he with the help of the War Goddess and his brother Angus, stopped the four remaining Fomorians of Ireland from spoiling the crops, and thus drove them out of the country for

PVR. MiDen.

ever. Following this event the Goddess issued a prophesy stating that the Tuatha De Danann were coming to the end of a divine age, and that the new era would have flowerless Summers, milkless cows, men would become weak, trees fruitless and in general all forms of rectitude would cease to exist. This divine prediction was to become as expected very true. The Tuatha De Danann were to be later invaded by the sons of the God Bile, who were themselves the ancestors of the Gaels.

On a spiritual level these new invading forces the Milesians may be seen to represent an incoming season as the Goddess prophesy suggests. The Milesians to the Tuatha De Danann (whether seen as a race of Gods or people) would bring into the Isle famine and death, or to put it into a nutshell - Winter. Just like the Fomorians they would be seen as everything that was unjust and bad. To the Milesians the Tuatha De Danann would of course be seen in exactly the same light as a dark enemy to be defeated.

The early Irish annalists regarded the battle between the resident Tuatha De Danann and invading Milesians as being a struggle 'twixt Gods and men. The Milesian push eventually drove the Tuatha De Danann into exile beneath the Earth, following two epic skirmishes fought at Glenn Faisi and Tailtiu (Telltown) in both of which the Gods were defeated. Although they had been dispossessed of the upper earth the Gods continued to be troublesome to the Milesians. Many surviving Celtic myths and legends lead us to the realisation that the exiled underworld Gods took on the embodiment of the cosmic natural forces in river, mountain, wood and glen - both creative and destructive.

It was thought to be most essential for wise mortals to respect the old Gods in order for the crops to grow well and the cattle to produce milk. The Gods had in effect become the *'fairy people'* of the Sidhe or underground barrows or

APOLLO. PUR 95

hillocks, each of which was an entrance to the underworld realm of great pleasures and delights. These underhill kingdoms were granted to each of the Gods by the Dagda who was now their leader, he himself had two, both in close proximity to the River Boyne.

Mider dwelled in one called the Sidhe of Bri-Leith in County LongFord, in fact all the Tuatha De Danann were provided with these new underground homes. It is not difficult for anyone who has visited deep and mysterious caves to appreciate why the Celts believed these places to be the abodes of supernatural forces such as spirits or Gods. The magical charge of such sites has to be experienced and felt intuitively, this is not the realm of the analytical logical mind, and the Celts being much closer to Mother Earth than modern man, knew this instinctively.

The Roman sun God Apollo, brought here by the legions, was equated with the Celtic deity Lleu or Lugh. It must be remembered however that the British/Irish deity in question here was not originally a solar deity, as the Celts were not primarily farm settlers. The integration with Roman culture and religions was the likeliest cause for the later adoption of 'Sun' God worship amongst certain tribal units. Like his Celtic counterpart, Apollo was a God of many attributes - music, the arts, flocks and prophecy all fell under Apollo's jurisdiction. His image appears at intervals on the imperial coinage from Augustus to Aurelian. Lugh and Apollo follow remarkably similar lines in their capacity as Gods with solar characteristics, both regarded as being strong, just, handsome and skillful.

Lugh is still remembered during the Harvest festival of the 1st August - Lugnassad, which was re-dedicated by the Romans to Augustus, a time when the ripe yellow cornfields magically link to the golden hair of the 'many skilled' Lugh. Lugh's grandfather Balor was a King of the Fomorians, at

the second battle of Mag Tuireadh (Moytura) Lugh killed him by casting a magic stone which struck the old God fatally in the eye knocking it completely out. This event led to the Fomorians being driven into the sea and victory for the Tuatha De Danann.

The golden festival of Lugnassad marks such epic cycles in Celtic lore, Lugh as the shining young God of Summer, is seen to over-come and defeat the dangerous Fomorian older God, Balor who portrays the Winter season and time of decay. Although this festival is a joyous time of light associations, it is also a time to reflect upon the darker cool nights of Autumn to come.

As the ripening corn reaches it's long awaited zenith, welcome to the realisation that life and death are but two sides of the same coin. Soon the harvest is over, leaving only the empty stubble where once stood proud, full glowing fields of nature's rich bounty. By slaying his grandfather, Lugh actually kills a part of himself - a part that has to perish, like the over-ripe corn of Summer or the sinking mid-Winter sun. It has to be so in order for him to follow the relentless cosmic tides of life and death. This part of him, he has to sacrifice so as to bring forth the future new growth of a virgin Spring.

Modern Christians, will of course be quite unaware of the vast store-house of Pagan legend behind their adopted contemporary harvest festival (Lammas), whilst demoting vital deities like Lugh to the ranks of a Celtic hero or like the great Mother Goddess Brigit into a lowly Saint, not to be mentioned in the classroom for fear that students may be inquisitive or even start to investigate the real origins of their true Pagan birthright.

Lugh's Welsh equivalent was Llew Llaw Gyffes, son of Arianrhod. Llew was fostered by the God of magic Gwydion. In one legend Gwydion takes on the representation of

Venus

P.V.R. 95.

light/Summer by defeating in battle Pryderi - God of the underworld. Many tales of Gwydion's exploits were later absorbed into Arthurian myth and credited to Arthur himself. We can also draw parallels with the Norse/Saxon Odin or Woden here, and the Gaelic God of eloquence and writing Oghma. Odin, Oghma and Gwydion all had two important connections in common, namely magic and warfare.

At the height of their popularity the knowledge of writing would certainly have been considered as a magical talent possessed by very few enlightened individuals. The power to convey an idea or concept by merely carving marks on a rock or branch, would have imbued the skillful operator with an immense respect and reverence from other members of the tribe or clan. Odin is credited with discovering the runes whilst hanging inverted for nine days and nights upon the Norse cosmic tree - Yggdrasil.

Like many later deified personages, Odin was probably originally a tribe leader who may have actually been suspended as a punishment upon a forest tree a favoured mode of chastisement or execution amongst earlier Northern races. The floor of a sun-lit wood is a very magical place indeed, the flickering shadows eventually lull even the most hardened sceptic into a state of mystical trance, where the distorted boughs of an old broken Willow convey a twisted energy pattern, whilst a gentle Birch or Elder reflects the same tranquil light form as it's material counterpart.

These fragmented images then become concentrated to form the Runes, mirroring the same energies as the trees themselves thus the Runic Alphabet became not only a secular scholarly script, but also and more importantly, a way of delivering magical knowledge denied to all but the select few.

Oghma was credited with discovering the Ogham Alphabet. This script is similar to Roman numerals and there may be a connection here although the exact origin of this form of writing is not wholly proven. It is often wrongly suggested that such knowledge had to be restricted to the safe custody of the ruling priesthoods of the day, as such power was inherently dangerous.

This slight of hand merely gave the mystical monopoly to the spiritually elitist few, enabling them to control and dictate the religious policy of the day. Just as in contemporary society priestly castes have always sought to be an intermediary between a man and his God - each new theocracy claiming to be the only true way to salvation.

Modern Christian criticism of Tarot cards, crystal balls, the Runes and all Occultist methods, illustrates this point very clearly indeed. Society is hoodwinked into believing such items to be *'bad for the soul or evil'*, when the real problem lies with the ruling theocracy, who, being terrified of losing their religious grip on the nation stoop to inventing false spiritual scares, using fear as a key to ensure religious compliance of the naive masses. This is the way it has always been in the struggle for religious power over populations in general.

Myths of course get altered in many cases over the centuries, however as we have previously observed studying such ancient tales whilst *'reading between the lines'*, does indeed lead us to the revelation of discovering much of our pre-Christian indigenous heritage otherwise denied to us by modern theologians.

Odin, Gwydion and Oghma were not adverse to using armed force when they deemed it necessary. Oghma was a champion warrior of the Tuatha De Danann, his epitaph was Grianainech meaning *' sunny-faced '* which may suggest that

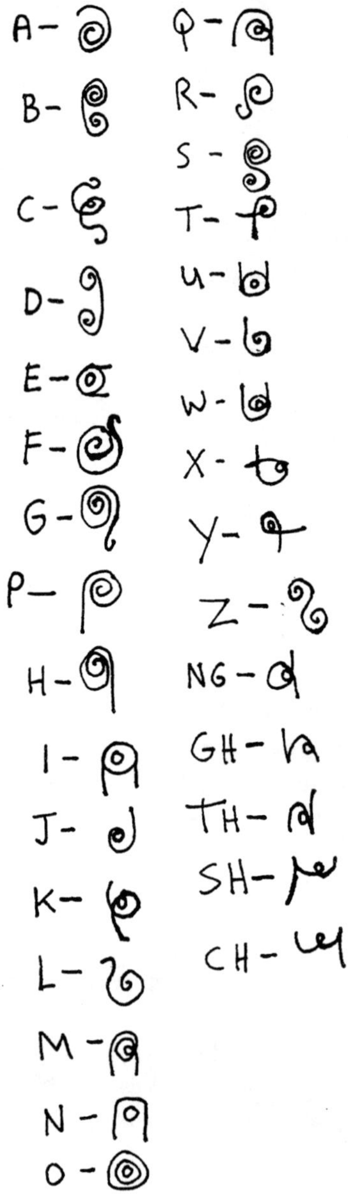

A— Q—
B— R—
     S—
C— T—
D— U—
E— V—
F— W—
G— X—
P— Y—
H— Z—
I— NG—
J— GH—
K— TH—
L— SH—
M— CH—
N—
O—

Pictish Script

Common Germanic Runes

= RUNE MARK.
= MODERN LETTER.

= RUNE MARK.
= MODERN LETTER.

= RUNE MARK.
= MODERN LETTER.

Rune Mark	ᚠ	ᚢ	Þ	ᚨ	ᚱ	ᚲ	ᚷ	ᚹ	ᚺ	ᚾ	ᛁ
Modern Letter	F	U	TH	A	R	K	G	W	H	N	I

Rune Mark											
Modern Letter	J	P	Z	S	T	B	E	M			

Rune Mark					
Modern Letter	Ng	O	D	L	

55

Ogham Beth Luis Nion Celtic Alphabet

he also had been revered with solar attributes like Lugh. His Father was the Dagda and Brigit was his sister, Oghma had engaged Lugh in a test of strength prior to the war with the Fomorian giants, a test that was to later lead to Lugh becoming commander of battle against the giants.

As personifications of all that was strong, true and noble in the human sphere, Oghma, Lugh and the Dagda were to later combine forces in a trinity of strength to lay siege on the Fomorians after the theft of the Dagda's harp. Dagda's harp represented the transformation of one season to another, the changing cycles of life and death. The Tuatha De Danann's quest to rescue the Dagda's stolen harp from Fomorian hands is an ancient Celtic narrative, which refers to the eternal conflict that exists between chaos and harmony. After finding the harp the Dagda sings and the instrument which then leaps from the wall, kills nine Fomorians then comes back to the Dagda - it's rightful owner.

Here we see a portrayal of the light God's victory over the dark giants, of natural cosmic order being again restored intact from the grasp of catastrophe. The harp itself becomes here the magical creative/destructive energy source of the universe; that subsists as the neutral power underlying all levels of existence. The Celts were intimately aware of this undulating tidal life-force, magic existed (and still does) in every river, stone and tree, every animate and inanimate form held it's own particular spirit or consciousness, similar yet subtly different to their own.

The Welsh Goddess - Don, was the mother of Gwydion, however later Christian writers converted her into a King of Dublin, who led the Irish into North Wales in A.D. 267. Such mythological demotions like this were common-place. Gods/Goddesses turned into Heroes, Saints, Kings, Queens or Devils. The reason for this type of alteration in Pagan myth and legend is quite obvious. Insidious moulding of old Pagan

'LUGH'

PVR 95.

deities into Kings and Heroes gave the Christian Fathers the vital means to an end. Rural Pagan folk accepted the modified legends readily, whilst not realising the subtle Christian twist that ensued the de-ranking of the very same deities once held by them in the highest esteem.

This in turn allowed the Eastern cult of Christianity to gain the foot hold it so badly craved. In 601 A.D. Pope Gregory instructed Abbot Mellitus to inform Bishop Augustine to destroy all Pagan idols in Britain. He also commanded that Pagan temples should be sanctified with holy water and re-dedicated to the service of Christ - on no account were they to be destroyed.

This was done to win over more converts to Christianity, a clever ploy that paid off. The populace still payed homage to their old sacred sites, whilst revering the new Christian deity. Earlier Pagan God forms were not however to be completely forgotten, many examples of Pagan sculpture still remain, to be seen in old churches, chapels and abbeys which would suggest that Christian theocracy was not always completely successful in subduing indigenous religious belief. One of the most common type of Bas reliefs was the Sheela-na- Gig, a squatting female figure with grotesquely enlarged genitals. It is obvious that the population of many regions paid the new monotheistic religion only *'lip-service'* as the popular use of such Pagan stonemasonry proved.

Unable to stamp on Pagan faith as thoroughly as they would have liked, Sheela-na-Gig's were quietly tolerated as good luck charms that might deflect evil spirits away from the house of God. The truth of the matter is that the Sheela-na-Gig's, coarse as they were, stood firmly in the native consciousness as a folk memory and reminder of what male dominated Christianity couldn't possibly hope to achieve, the essential aspect of female divinity, the great Earth Goddess herself.

THE DAGDA.   PUR.

The somewhat ugly images of the Sheela-na-Gig's bear a striking resemblance to fertility Goddess figurines found all over the world and from many different Pagan cultures. The Sheela-na-Gig represents the pre-Christian irrepressible celebration of human sexuality, a natural part of life that had to be expressed graphically. The great Earth Mother Goddess was seen as all embracing and this too is clearly displayed in the prominent sexual posture, so despised by later Christianisers with their hatred of the physical act of lovemaking.

It is likely that the Sheela figurines by-pass many eras in our history and form a link with an older native pre-Celtic folk religion. Similar neolithic Figurines have combined both male and female attributes such as bearded ladies or figures with breasts and penis. Neolithic thinking seems to have developed into a type of androgynous pattern following the later understanding of masculine necessity to complete the act of fertilisation, thus the bi-sexual combination of male and female divinity was encapsulated in single odd epicene images from which the Sheela figures may have later evolved.

The Sidhe fairy mounds/barrows inhabited by the Gaelic Gods may provide us with a meaning for our word Sheela (possibly an early translation) who opens her very self just as the Sidhe's open up on the night of Samhain - 31st October-1st November marking that important celebration - the start of the Celtic Winter.

Sheela-na-Gig may be a representation of the Goddess Danu, although her pedigree as stated above was most likely to be a great deal older, evidence perhaps defining Celtic adoption of indigenous religious systems. Samhain has been superficially Christianised as Hallowe'en/All Saints Day, however the festival itself remains as a potent reminder of our pre-Christian Pagan heritage. Celtic myths connected with

HERNE. PUR.

Samhain tell of the cosmic battle between the powers of light/dark, Summer/Winter. The people of Nemed struggled with the Fomorian Giants just as the Tuatha De Dannan had done later on. Samhain's associations with Winter/darkness led early Christianisers to portray this ancient Feast of the Dead as being a time of satanic evil. The Pagan Celts did not have Satan as part of their religious symbolism or beliefs, this personification of ultimate evil is a wholly Christian invention unlike dualistic Christianity.

The Celts realised that one had to have a vital balance between light/dark, one couldn't exist without the other. The early church twisted and influenced native culture converting 'horned Gods' that innocently represented the masculine fert- ilising aspect of nature into the evil figure of Satan, an image that still remains today as a reminder of our loss of native wisdom.

The horns that once stood proud on the Stag, Ram and Bull as a symbol of life and strength were to become the Christian representation of that spiritual scapegoat for man's troubles and ills the Devil. This mythological conversion of materialistic evil in nature proved decisive in destroying native Pagan culture all around the globe.

Many ancient pre-Christian societies revered horned deities. The Celts had Cernunnos, the Greeks and Romans had Pan, many other examples existed all reflecting the vigorous procreative life-force essential to evolution on Earth, unfortunately it was an easy task for rabid medieval zealots throughout the dark ages to cry 'the devil has horns so all communities containing this image must be satanic!'.

One of the most enduring legends involving the horned God aspect of masculine divinity is that of the 'wild hunt', a phantasmal horseman leading a pack of baying hounds through the night air. The Welsh Gwynn ap Nudd (son of

Nudd) is a deity that was believed to lead the pack in Wales and the West of England. Further South we have the character of *'Herne the Hunter'* an antler horned British God that haunts Windsor Great Park at midnight. Cernunnos is the Gaulish/British original prototype of Herne, his worship was brought into Britain by Belgic settlers.

Romano-Gaulish figures often feature the deities Apollo and Cernunnos seated side by side, so the horned God certainly was extremely popular even with non-indigenous races. It would be highly inaccurate to assume that horned deities didn't exist before the Belgic tribes arrived here, as the British Isles contained Stags, Cattle, goats, all animals sporting horns or antlers. Early neolithic hunters certainly linked with the magical energies of the Stag in order to fully understand the inherent life force flowing from their expected quarry. The Shamanistic stag dance of modern North American Indians illustrates what the ancient British hunters would have been like admirably. It was vital for these early people to magically *'become'* the stag - to take on its spirit form before the hunt, to ensure a successful outcome.

Later in the mythological cycle of things, horned Gods took on the role of guardians of the Underworld and war. Cernunnos as Lord of all horned animals and the wild hunt, sweeps the souls of the dead into Annwn (the Celtic Hades). The Northern Celtic war God was called Belatucadros and he was very popular with the people in the location of Cumbria. This deity was depicted as a horned God like Cernunnos.

In Wales the God Beli was the grandfather of Lleu Llaw Gyffes. Beli equated with the Gaelic Balor. The concept of the wild hunt and it's eerie leader, of whichever name, is a representation of the terror brought by disease, plague or ultimately death, the Grim Reaper claiming his deadly toll. Incidentally, the Norse Odin who as a deity of death was also known as Grimr (the hooded one) as in Grimsby (Grims town/ homestead), led to the title Grim Reaper.

The pack of hounds that accompanied the wild hunt had various names in different localities. In Lancashire and Yorkshire they were known as Ratchets or Gabriel Hounds, in Wales they are the Cwn-Annwn (Hounds of the Underworld), in Devonshire they become the Wisht or Yeth Hounds. Of course in the physical sense hunting and death go hand in hand, so it is quite easy to see why these two subjects become synonymous. On the material level it could also be thought that the lonely calls of migrating Pink Foot or Grey Lag geese in the cold Winter night's sky led to such legends as the wild hunt. Even the eerie song of the wolf or fox could be underlying such tales.

The origins of the wild hunt seems to equate with the cry of the Banshee in some ways, and it is possible that the more sensitive or psychically attuned Shamans of earlier native cultures linked intimately with the Earth cycles, observed the changing moods and fluxs of planetary events, and instinctively knew when death (i.e. the wild hunt), was at hand. This illogical, instinctive common wisdom that is really very *'uncommon'* now and is the reason why so many often unintelligible myths/legends prove so hard to fathom out, when examined only on a logical/conscious level of thought. Looking at mythology with scientific eyes only leads to a certain definitive understanding of cultural belief, but this understanding will be limited to *'material'* wisdom.

The true *'knowing'* in a magical sense is experienced in the feel of the lapping Spring tide on bare feet, the heat of the June sun glancing warmly off the shoulders in a forest glade, the power of a December blizzard driving hard against one's face, and the quiet unease felt at midnight in a dense woodland fog in Autumn. It is said that the nearer the wild hunt is to a man, the farther off they sound, and conversely

PUR.

HERNE -
'LORD OF THE
WILDWOOD'

the hounds are far away when they seem to be close at hand. This prompts the analogy with the old maxim 'can't see wood for trees', in other words when a thing is in close proximity to you, it becomes invisible or insignificant.

On the other hand anyone familiar with flat beaches will know how strange it seems to clearly hear a conversation between distant people, even up to a mile away on a calm day with the breeze coming at you, every word is perfectly audible, and you could swear that the conversationalists were only a few yards away. It is feasible that this hypothesis on the night sounds of the wild hunt goes some way to explaining such a question. The Lord of the Dead and his spirit hounds represent the awesome dark forces of stormy nights when the wise man avoided straying too far away from the security of his hearth.

The God of Winter, archery and hunting in the Northern cultures was called Uller, he was known as Vulder to the Anglo-Saxons. In areas of Germany he was called Holler (perhaps the root of the name Holland). This God like Odin was believed to lead a wild hunt, he was also adept in the use of runes. Uller endured the warm Summer months with the Goddess Hel in the Underworld, giving way to Odin, who in this instance was seen as the Lord of Summer. Here again we observe the immortal combat of light and dark displayed in the grandure of mythological treatise.

It is interesting to note that with the advent of Christianity, characters like King Arthur, Herod, certain Swedish Kings and various other secular personages were assigned the role of leaders of the hunt, this was obviously implanted in the native consciousness by church authorities who realised that suppression of the Pagan wild hunt legend (and other myths), was not nearly so effective as exchanging Heathen deities for semi-divine or historical personalities. This ensured that the populace would eventually be swayed away

PUR. GRIMR.

from their true indigenous Pagan faith and deities, thus allowing the doctrine of Christianity to eradicate folk memory of earlier beliefs then and in future generations to come.

In British mythology one of the most endearing legends concerning the wild hunt involves the Welsh Gods of Annwn. Pwyll - a prince of Dyfed (S/W Wales), whilst out hunting with his hounds heard the cry of another pack approaching him. He saw a stag pulled down by these strange hounds with bodies of pure white hair and bright red ears. Pwyll didn't notice any riders with the hounds so he called his own pack to the quarry. Suddenly a horseman riding a grey steed, dressed in hunting attire came up to Pwyll and reprimanded him for his bad sportsmanship and discourtesy in claiming the kill for himself. Pwyll apologised to the stranger and asked his name,*"Arawn - King of Annwn"* came the reply.

In penance for his violation against Arawn, Pwyll was implored to visit Annwn and fight Havgan (a rival King of Annwn), who wanted to have Arawn's kingdom for himself. Pwyll agreed to complete this task, and he did this in the guise of Arawn himself. So good was the disguise that even Arawn's own wife failed to notice the difference. Similarly, Arawn took on the form of Pwyll. Pwyll in his disguise, spent a part of the year in the realm of Annwn enjoying great merriment.

On the allotted day of battle, Pwyll slew Havgan as expected - then rejoined Arawn, after which they both resumed their original forms once again. Later Arawn explained to his baffled wife the nature of events, and they all agreed that the bond between Annwn and Dyfed was strong indeed. Pwyll was, following this adventure given the new title of Head of Annwn.

In this particular myth, Pwyll represents the spirit of the land of Dyfed, he is sought out by Arawn-Lord of the Underworld who is unable to quell the chaotic forces of Havgan, and needs an ally.

This is a story of transitional magic, Pwyll journeys into the Underworld in order to bring harmony to the troubled land by defeating Havgan, who personifies all that is negative and dangerous. We see here shades of the battle between Gwen and Gwyrthur for Creudylad, which is of course Winter's grip meeting Summer for the prize that is Spring.

In Pwyll's story the reward is not a maiden like Creudylad, but the peace and prosperity of the land that reflects the image of Spring, the land itself being the great Earth Mother, Arawn and Havgan are in many ways one and the same character - a positive and negative polarity in one deity. Arawn realises that he needs help to overcome the dark sinister aspect of himself in order to promote future growth and make himself whole, thus Pwyll's necessary magical influence is brought to Annwn. By venturing into Annwn, Pwyll brings life out of death, he personifies the magical force that leads to reincarnation and new life - he brings order where before only chaos reigned.

The Hounds of Annwn with their white and red appearance are common in Celtic myths. Their colouration reminds the observer that they are indeed of a magical nature and not of the material realm. The Stag with its magical connection to the great horned God Cernunnos needs no introduction. This fabulous creature leads Pwyll into the Underworld and represents the power of magical transformation.

Anybody who regularly visits a Northern spate river surrounded by dense woodland, will eventually gain an affinity for the legend of Pwyll's quest. I often visit the River Hodder in the Trough of Bowland - Lancashire. The stream is reached some half a mile down a steep wooded hillside, if one is very quiet a Stag or Hind may occasionally be seen coming through the Oak and Alders down to the water to drink. However one small sound and they run swiftly away, leaving only the meandering silver stream to keep one company. Best of all is to sight a Stag coming out of the mist early on a Summer's morning - evoking the beautiful living mystery of the native folk legends themselves.

All the myths of these lovely Isles reflect the Celtic deep love and vast understanding of nature's many and changing moods, moods that also move through and with us. We all have the inherent ability to link with the energies exhibited in myth and legend, because indirectly the tales of old are still about us, we contain within ourselves the very same forces of nature so nobly portrayed in myth. To understand legendary tales is to understand oneself and this is one of mythology's most valuable gifts to mankind, (i.e. self knowledge). It is not even necessary to be a professor of history, mythology, language, or any subject, to learn a rudimentary appreciation of the old tales, all one needs is an open mind and a love of nature. Best of all, get into the wild countryside (there's still some left) and find your own sacred sites. You will know such places intuitively - they will feel right. Forget the map and get out there, drink in that natural energy force just like your ancestors did, and experience it as it is.

The saga of Pwyll, Arawn and Havgan appealed to later Norman Christian Romancers who adopted it into the tale of the battle between Gawain and his fearsome opponent - the Green Knight. Many other such epics were taken up by the later writers of Arthurian legends, which is not at all surprising as each new culture, Saxon to Norman, Celt to Roman, Gael to Iberian, observed, adapted, then ultimately converted the older mythos to suit it's own exclusive taste.

'LORD OF THE MOUNTAIN'

PVR.

King Arthur has been credited as Leader of the Wild Hunt, and he actually takes on many of the divine deity attributes of Gwydion, Gwyn, Odin and Herne. There seems also to have been a historical King Arthur who was given the task of being a type of roving Commander in charge of Britain's defence following the withdrawal of Rome's troops in AD 410, by the Emperor Honorius. Following the departure of the legions, Britain was to be increasingly subjected to a new and brutal threat - the Saxons.

The Anglo-Saxon Goddess of fertility and the Spring was called Ostara/Eostre and devotion to her was so great that later Christian theologians saw fit to adopt her Spring festival (Easter) and claim it for their own. Ostara's Nordic counterpart Frigga or Freya was to unfortunately receive a less honourable fate.

Freya was often depicted driving a chariot pulled by two black cats and this single fact, was to be used by cruel mediaeval inquisitors during the witch-hunt hysteria. As they saw it Freya was a demoness, so individuals under suspicion of Witchcraft/sorcery were indeed guilty by association if they posse- ssed a black cat. This archetypal witches' familiar symbol was to lead many innocent victims to the blazing stake or hangman's noose!

The festival of the Spring Equinox, although important to the Teutonic/Saxon peoples had not been of great relevance to the earlier Celtic folk. Spring celebration and it's solar attributes of night and day being in equal balance, would have been marked readily by the ancient agricultural megalithic peoples. It was extremely important for them to link intimately with solar force, the very energy essential for the success of crops and the land that they depended on.

The Celts, as roaming cattle rearers, would later become aware of the vital necessity represented by the Sun's

OSTARA.

PVR.95.

indispensable power, following their increasing progression into the ways of the corn/wheat grower. Because of these issues it is true to say that Spring celebration was once a native tradition, then with Celtic invasion it declined - only later to again start a fresh revival with Roman and Teutonic influence.

This tidal ebbing and flowing of mythological thought, has caused a great deal of confusion in the understanding of our native deities and their true functions. This hypothesis may hopefully shed some light on why the misunderstanding occurred in the first place. Solar celebrations like the Equinoxes and Solstices fall into such a category as mentioned above, and this is why deities with solar associations and attributes (as in the God Lugh), have been in the past the source of so much misinterpretation at the hands of later mythologists.

The Roman God Mars, was revered during Spring and this deity was of particular importance, because he was believed to be the father of Romulus and Remus (founders of Rome), thus Romans called him Marspiter - Father Mars and thought themselves descended from him. Mars shared a festival called the Quinquatrus at the Spring Equinox with Minerva - Goddess of Arts and Craftsmen. The sacred attributes of Mars were a blazing torch and a spear, moreover in ancient Rome tradition the priests of Mars (or his Greek counterpart Ares), would advance before the legions carrying these symbols, to warn the opposing army to prepare for battle.

Nowadays we tend to think of the mediaeval knights' joust, when remembering the origins of chivalry, however the priests of Mars would seem to have been including such honourable manners in combat, many years previous to the English noblemen. Mars of course gives us the name of the month March (Martius), an important month in the agricultural year. The reason for this month being associated with a war God is because Mars was originally a God of the crops and Spring. The transition here is common throughout many cultures, and marks man's progress and development from the earliest neolithic times. Deities initially personified the elements and primordial forces experienced in nature.

Next came Gods of the hunt - horned Gods who depicted the fertilising aspect vital for life.Many early horned deities later became Gods of war simply because society had advanced to a stage where boundaries became important to survival. Clans and tribal units would drift apart and it was unavoidable that cultural conflicts would ensue. The Gods reflected man's sociological attunement to the world and era that he existed in. Man's ability to relate to deeper evolving subconscious thought processes with - in himself, became represented in the personified image of divinity. All and every part of the known and indeed the unknown world in which he lived, was given it's spiritual counterpart which in turn, allowed the worshipper an intimate relationship, with that particular single aspect of the essential divine whole.

The wife/sister of Mars was called Bellona, she had a sacred shrine at York (Eboracum) and a feast day on 24th March, which seems to suggest that like Mars, she had agricultural links. Bellona may equate with the Celtic War Goddess the Morrigu, as her delight in savage battle was also well known. The essential male/female balance in Pagan religious thought, is seen here again - a God has to be accompanied by a Goddess, man has to have woman. Cultures that persist with monotheistic male or indeed female dogma, eventually invite suppression, alienation, corruption and ultimately ruination, when the balance is eroded the end usually follows close at hand, waiting in the wings like the oncoming storm.

The spiritual starvation experienced by women in male hierarchies is a persistent form of mind control, that ensures in the short term, masculine superiority. The backlash of outraged femininity in this society such as, Votes for Women. The Feminist Movement and Christian women priests, is evidence of a dawning realisation of divine injustice. Women are starting to ask for the divine principle of femininity - the Goddess, although in many cases they probably don't even realise this.

Dogmatic priesthoods have always and will always place their own sense of authority and self importance before the best interests of their religious adherents, just like self-righteous politicians do. This principle applies to all faiths and unfortunately not only state approved ones at that.

Contemporary Paganism has it's own share of priesthoods, that should be promoting the individual's own personal link to the Goddess, but instead they themselves having failed to achieve a personal level of self initiation/knowledge, try to mask their own transparent inadequacies by surrounding themselves in mystic media - friendly auras and titles.

There will always be those in every religious system new or old, that seek power and self promotion above all else. This is the dark side of human nature, such suppressive mind control against individual religious experience and freedom, is as old as the hills. Power seekers in Greek, Roman, Egyptian, British, Indian and all other cultures have at certain periods in history, sought to introduce repressive measures to ensure compliance to their own particular brand of religion - promoting the worship of one particular deity (of their choice) above all others, using titles like *'All father' 'All Mighty' 'Unconquered'* etc. - to further their religious monopoly over the unsuspecting population.

The officialisation of religious thought is an extremely dangerous development for any society, and frequently precedes warfare. It marks the *'them against us'* type of

MARS. PUR.

nationalism such as that which was clearly displayed, during the Crusades of Richard the Lionheart and subsequent Jewish persecutions that occurred in England. At this particular time Jews were the sole bankers in England, and were despised for their exactions. Following Richard's coronation Jews approached his palace for protection, but were instead brutally murdered. The masses thereafter assumed the right to plunder and kill the innocent Jewish minorities throughout Britain.

It is a sad fact that some individuals 'hell bent' on promoting their own brand of suppressive spiritual doctrine, care nothing for the damage they create against others in society. This is how the sinister aspect of human nature has always surfaced, and as we all know intolerance leads to persecution which ultimately ends in genocide. The concept of genocide itself has been depicted in many deities throughout history, and primarily as the God/Goddess of war. The dark primordial force of destruction creates it's own grim reality, and our ancestors knew it only too well.

Boudicca - Queen of the Iceni invoked the Goddess of Victory; Andraste, during her fierce campaigns against the Romans in AD60. She had absolutely no other choice under the circumstances but to summon up divine devastation. Her late husband Prasutagus had left no son and heir, moreover his treaty had lapsed, so slaves from the Roman procuratorial office arrived to seize the property. During the fracas Boudicca was flogged and her daughters raped. The famous rebellion followed resulting in the wronged Queen sacking the towns of London, Colchester and Verulanium (St. Albans).

Boudicca's invocations to the Warrior Goddess obviously proved to be extremely successful as the uprising against Roman injustice spread like wild fire. The Trinovantes and other Celtic tribes were to soon join the Iceni rebels in their

'THE HARE'

P.V.R.

cause. Unfortunately Boudicca was later to be defeated by Roman leadership and greater discipline, under the authority of Suetonius Paulinus. To his credit he had only approximately 10,000 men whilst the Iceni Queen had twenty three times that number.

Suetonius chose a battlefield to his military advantage and with superior armament and discipline won the day. His Legio XIV and XX received high honours for their courageous stand against seemingly overwhelming odds, incredibly 80,000 British fell to only 400 Roman troops.

It was widely reported that Boudicca released a hare from the folds of her clothing at the height of the Iceni uprising as a rite of propitiation. The hare itself was possibly held to be sacred to Andraste. Boudicca would, by watching which way the hare travelled, deduce the best avenue of attack or defence, this was in fact a ritual of time honoured divination.

Hares have been considered by many cultures to be connected with the Moon and believed to hold the power of transformation. There is a great deal of common sense in this, as animals are much more psychically attuned to nature's cycles than most humans. They sense danger and act accordingly taking evasive actions long before we become aware of it, and of course the wise old Celts realised this truth. Boudicca's hare actually transformed her indecisiveness into positive military action - it's fear and native cunning became her power and strength.

The Goddess Andraste was probably linked to the Moon because of Boudicca's association with the 'lunar' hare and divination. Could Andraste have equated with the Gaelic Danu Anu? The answer is likely to be yes. It is also feasible that Andraste could have had a link with Astarte/Ashtart the Phoenician/Syrian Goddess of war, fertility and the moon. Incidentally Astarte is the Canaanite version of Ishtar, the

ANDRASTE

P.V.R.

major Assyro/Babylonian Earth Goddess and Ishtar's father was the Sky God Anu.

It seems doubtful that the Gaelic Anu and this Eastern Anu are connected, however many far Eastern deities were found to have temples or shrines in Britain (there was an altar dedicated to Astarte at Corbridge) so we need to keep an open mind.

The hare has been seen by many cultures as a symbol of procreation and elemental existence, it was sacred to the Greek lunar Goddess Hecate and this is not surprising, as the hare is a mainly nocturnal creature becoming increasingly active when the moon's pale light casts silent shadows across the meadows. The strange antics of male hares engaged in Spring rivalry for a female partner also adds to it's association with the lunar cycle, magic and mystery.

Many legends of the hare's transitional qualities will have originated from its peculiar habit of lying very still in hiding, then when approached suddenly springing up and darting away. In olden times corn reapers would frequently observe a hare swiftly dash from out of the last bushel of uncut corn. This event was seen as the spirit of the corn itself, actually leaving the fields in the transformal image of a hare. Boudicca's rite of divination with the hare would, because of the hare's divine associations appear to be also a direct appeal for assistance to the Goddess Andraste. If Andraste was indeed a lunar deity as suggested, then Boudicca must have sought to connect with her dark aspect, the terrible mother/war Goddess, linking to the moon's dark quarter.

The hare's divinary usage by the Icenian Queen, also ties up with unification to Goddess principles, as prophecy is usually connected to the mystery of the great mother herself - *she who knew, knows, and will know what is to pass '*. Andraste must be seen as a very important deity encompassing many various aspects of life. Although depicted as a warrior death-dealing Goddess, she was hailed as the personification of righteousness and victory over Roman oppression by the Iceni - without her influence they would have been a vastly inferior force, and easy prey for the might of the legions. Because of the closely approaching tide of Christian influence, the epic Iceni rebellion remained as an historical event only.

It is most likely that this tale of great courage would have taken on mythological connotations if Christian chroniclers had not later imposed restrictive mind control measures on the populace. Boudicca may have later gained semi-divine stature or even attained complete deification, as many earlier historical personages had. The British forces could have been portrayed as Summer conquering the hard biting Roman Winter or vice versa of course, to the Roman mind. In many ways Boudicca's revolt was our last chance of mythological greatness, but this was not to be. Boudicca's saga of British resistance seems to have assimilated certain aspects of the Celtic sovereign Goddess Britannia/Brigantia myth. Stubborn British pride, the Bulldog breed, and Britain's Never Never Will Be Slaves, (Rule Britannia!), all these idioms/sentiments have interconnections with Boudicca, so perhaps she has in some respects gained the ennoblement she so richly deserved.

One interesting character legend who gained semi-divine status was Finn Mac Coul. Finn was the leader of the Fenians, a kind of Autochthonous Irish military reserve force, similar in fashion to the British Arthur, who was thought to have been given command of Britain following the Roman withdrawal of 410 AD. Finn and his Fenians appeared in numerous mythological stories, their first objective was to defend the coasts of Ireland against foreign conquest. In the six months of Winter the Fenians were given refuge by the populace, however during Summer they were believed to fend for themselves outdoors, by hunting wild animals and catching their own fish.

This seasonal clue to the Fenians exploits would suggest that they were here being portrayed not only as a possibly historical type of Home Guard, but also as an ancient personification of the annually changing forces of nature.

It is highly likely that the historical Finn and his brave band of warriors were moulded on the legendary Tuatha De Danann. Being a Fenian was not just a matter of prowess with sword and shield, on the contrary a Fenian was expected to show skill as a poet, musician and Bard. This cultural expertise reminds us of the attributes given to members of the Tuatha De Danann, and amounts to further proof of the Fenians representation as natural cosmic forces. Finn was kind, gentle and truthful, always eager to assist those in distress just like the legendary King Arthur, and this aspect of Finn indicates that he depicts a beneficent power, the force of natural growth.

Finn's father was called Camhal - a name which fuses with the Celtic War/Sky God Camulos, who in turn gives his name to the Roman town of Camulodunum (Colchester). Incidentally the 'Old King Cole' rhyme links with this deity and town as the mythical British Coel - Duke of Caer-Coelvin. Shakespeare's Cymbeline was based upon the Belgic King Cunobelinus who reigned for 40 years, Colchester being also known as the royal town of Cunobeline.

Colchester (Camulodunum) was the first Roman town in Britain, the Roman Emperor - Claudius founded a 'Colonia' at this location after conquering the South/Eastern part of the island. This place was sacred to the Celtic tribe called the Trinovantes and it formed their capital settlement.

ANDRASTE. PUR.

This is no doubt because of it's strategic importance for military defence. It was protected by the convergence of two valleys and surrounded by defensive dykes, no wonder it was named after *'Camulous'* the *'War God!'* Finn's father Camhal was, as stated, a sky/battle deity, and his connection with Camulos the Celtic God will also no doubt conjoin with the King Camulos, of the Tuatha De Danann fame.

Pagan myths and historical personages cross over and intertwine, turning heroes into Gods and Gods in turn into heroes. The historical Finn obviously like many other famous individuals later took on divine associations, however in some instances the reverse is true. Early Christian annalists worked hard and in general succeeded well in belittling many Pagan legends by twisting Gods into heroes, thereby reducing their original divine nature, into mere humanised glory. Because of this, the wise person should always be extremely suspicious of *'old hero stories'* that may in fact have originated as evidence of ancient pre-Christian religious belief systems.

Finn gained his powers when he was a young man. One day whilst walking along the banks of the River Boyne, he came upon an old master of the magical arts who was attempting to catch one of the *'Salmons of Knowledge'*. Shortly after meeting Finn, the old man succeeded in landing his coveted fish. He warned Finn not to eat any part of it, however whilst cooking the prized fish, Finn unfortunately burnt his thumb and without thinking proceeded to ease the pain by sucking it.

The old man was displeased with Finn, but on learning Finn's true name his disappointment turned to gladness, for he had prophesied that one named Finn would eventually come and capture a Salmon of Knowledge. The old man was also called Finn, and he had laboured for seven years trying to land a fish without success, obviously believing that the fish because of his name, would be his alone. Following this venture, the young Finn could magically foretell the future by putting his thumb to his mouth, just as he had when he'd scalded it in the old man's cooking pot.

That amazing fish - the Salmon represented universal wisdom and it is not at all surprising that the Celtic mind found this beautiful creature so mystical. Adult Salmon start life in fresh water rivers, then after becoming smolts they migrate to the wild ocean. After spending up to five years in the Sea feeding heavily, they return to the same river of their birth, surmounting many difficult obstacles to reach the spawning grounds. The Salmon does not feed at all following it's arrival in the river system, and this alone must have been enough for the Celts to grant this incredible fish mystical symbolism.

How could such a large fish weighing possibly over 60 lbs never have any food in it's stomach after capture in the river or stream? Obviously to Celtic thinking, it must be a creature of divine wisdom, so by eating it - one could partake in the same divine energy source, gain great knowledge and magical prowess. Contemporary Salmon anglers will, without knowledge of the mythological background of their quarry, never be able to appreciate why they are so awestruck with the sheer majesty of this fabulous beast.

As I said, the Salmon represents the aspect of universal wisdom, however on a deeper level, the Salmon is symbolic of a dream quest, a journey into the oceanic depths of the human unconscious mind, and the truths therein. Finn's power gained from this fish, equates indirectly with the young King Arthur's acquisition of the sword Excalibur - another symbol of wisdom and energy. The sword of Arthur, of course also has an affinity with water, hence it's association with the Lady of the Lake. Water represents the magical power of transformation. Without it all life perishes.

Overnight rain turns arid desert into green pasture and a lazy Summer stream is transformed by a downpour, into a raging torrent that allows the Autumn Salmon to once again return to the river of its ancestral birth. The Celts knew these truths, they also undoubtedly realised that water was the realm of the universal mother - the great Goddess herself - reason enough to explain why creatures like the fantastic Salmon were deemed so very wise and knowledgeable.

Perhaps the modern Salmon fisherman contains a remnant of this Celtic reverence for his prey, why else would he spend so much time pursuing such a frustrating, elusive, non-feeding fish as this? Angling for Salmon is notoriously difficult, involving many futile hours, days, weeks, even months without the single offer of a fish. However the dedication and persistent qualities of these anglers is uncanny, they fish relentlessly for that one slim chance against all odds, often refusing the opportunity to catch a more obliging species in favour of that one 'magical' Salmon. Possibly the above hypothesis explains their tenacious stubbornness to some extent, and puts the common title 'King of Fish' into some understandable perspective.

Finn's Salmon of Knowledge was one of several that had originated from a 'magical well' that later was to become the River Boyne. These Salmon had previously eaten nuts from nine sacred Hazel trees that overhung the well. The crimson nuts contained knowledge of all things.

This particular story is an Irish version of the Hebrew myth of the Tree of Knowledge, the number nine being in Hebrew symbolic of truth. Nuts depict future growth, occult wisdom and patient waiting, the crimson colour attributed to the nuts may suggest a fusion with other legends involving not the Hazel, but the Rowan or Mountain Ash which sports bright red berries, whereas the Hazel's nuts tend to be pinkish-brown in colour.

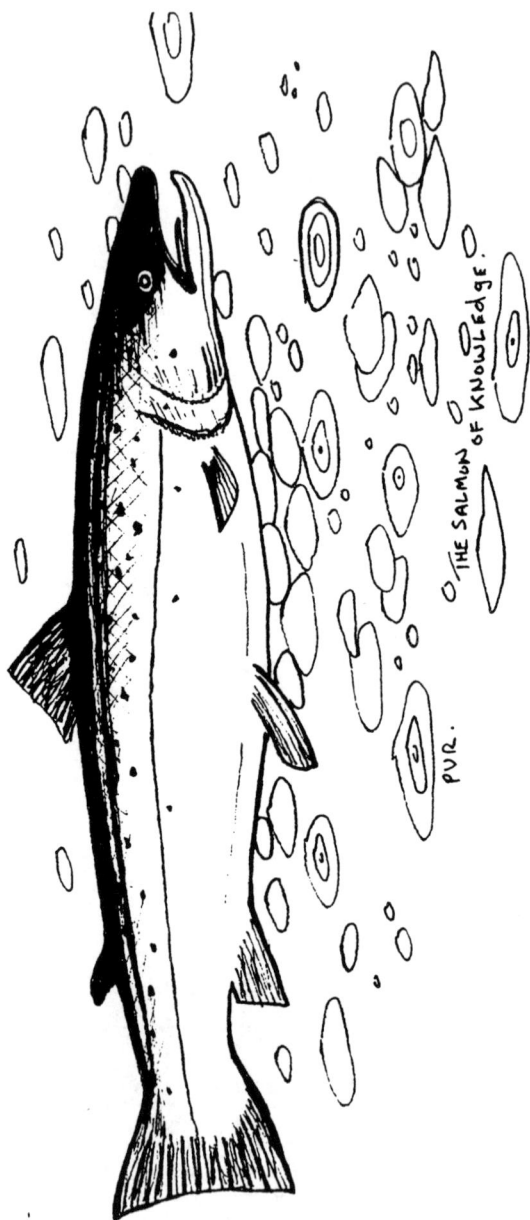

THE SALMON OF KNOWLEDGE.

PVR.

The Rowan was known as the *'magic quicken tree'*, and it's fruit were called the ambrosia of the Gods because they were believed to impart immortality. Whether originally Hazel or Rowan is really of no consequence here, as bright red/crimson is symbolic of life and growth.

Displayed for all to see in the majesty of the rising sun, the berries magically link with the increasing solar energy therein. It is not surprising that the early Christian chroniclers worked overtime to give native Pagan myth a subversive Christian slant. Many seemingly indigenous flood stories are blatant Christianisations, implanted on the masses to gain more converts to the Eastern religion of Christ.

Various colonisers of Ireland were described as coming from *'Spain'*, however this is a post-Christian euphemism for the Celtic otherworld. By merely swopping a single word like this, the missionary activists succeeded in subconsciously denying future generations access to their own native spiritual origins. Spain is a geological place, so once this slight of hand was accepted by the population, the new but alien concept of Christian Heaven/Hell could then be introduced, thereby stamping monotheism onto sacred native culture. This fact may appear small and insignificant at first, however it is essential to realise that this single missionary tactic has been responsible for the loss of numerous Pagan cultures, and lead to the evangelisation of many more all over the globe.

Gwyn ap Nudd British God of the Underworld also received the missionary treatment. He was reduced to being King of the Fairies, and previously he was said to control a nest of demons in Annwn. This mention of demons/devils instantly tells us that we are here observing Christianisation of Pagan myth actually taking place.

GWYN AP NUDD

The devil or Satan of course being alien to Pagan belief and an invention of Christian dualist thinking. Gwyn deserved a much better fate than this, as this deity was the highly venerated son of the Sky/River God Nudd or Nodens. There is a shrine of Nodens at Lydney Park in Gloucestershire on the River Severn, where a *'curse tablet'* was uncovered. It was dedicated to Nodens by a Pagan named Silvanus, who being irate at having his precious ring stolen, saw fit to seek help from the God, to ensure its safe return.

At Uley in the Cotswolds similar tablets have been found, some having Roman names, others Celtic, one dedicated by a lady is seeking the assistance of the Roman God Mercury, to help recover lost linen! Nodens received his title from Roman hands, originally this deity was called Nudd by the Welsh and Nuada by the Irish. Nuada was at first a King of the Tuatha De Danann who, having lost his hand at the battle of Moytura, had a silver replacement fashioned by the Celtic God of healing - Diancecht.

To the Roman conquerors Nodens must have been an extremely important deity. He was depicted as a strong youth (like Apollo) steering a chariot pulled by four powerful horses, he appears with a halo suggesting solar associations and flying elementals representing the four winds. Nodens as a Sky God probably impressed the Romans as being very similar to their supreme God-Jupiter.

The fourth day of the week, Thursday (Thors-day) is given in planetary occultist symbolism to Jupiter, so the four horses and four winds would of course fit in nicely with an equation between Nodens and Jupiter. Nodens being a deity with a temple site on the banks of a river where people like the angry Silvanus invoked the Gods help, to punish wrong doers, gives another clue to his Jupiter-like affinity.

MERCURY.

P.V.R.95.

94

In Rome one of Jupiter's sterner functions was to mete out justice to perjurers, so could Nodens too have been in fact the personification of divine justice, or even vengeance against law-breakers ?

The site at Lydney Park gets it's name from Nodens other alias (i.e. Llud or Lud), and Llud also gives his name to the various titles of London including - Ludesgate (Saxon) and Parth Llud by the Britons. The God Llud was like many other deities, converted by later annalists into a mythical King of Britain particularly by Geoffrey of Monmouth and Lady Charlotte Guest in her famous *Mabinogion*.

It is tempting to be critical of all romancers who change indigenous Pagan deities into lesser beings, however one must realise that when these mythological conversions were taking place, the prevalent political/religious climate of the time, may have proved to be too restrictive to print the true factual accounts of ancient Gods.

In many ways the old chroniclers have done us a favour, even with their sometimes obviously intentional desire to mask the old Gods. By stripping away the paper thin veneer of Christian *'God into King or hero romance'*, we can again discover the rich Pagan heritage that lies dormant just waiting for us to uncover. If it were not for the aberrations of ancient legend by romancers like the Christian Normans, then it may have been that the very mythological stepping stone connecting us to our native deities, could have been lost forever.

Jupiter and Nodens as Gods of the sky, water and thunder, have a great deal in common with the Norse Thunder God, Thor. As we already know Thor gives us the name of Thursday, and this 4th day is also Jupiter's day. Jupiter is frequently depicted holding a thunder bolt, whilst Thor carries his mighty hammer *'Mjolnir'* which is of course the

JupiTER   P.V.R. 95.

Nordic equivalent of the same element of thunder. Ancient peoples held the elemental forces of nature in great awe.

The terrifying and sudden roar of a thunder storm crashing loudly in a vast fiord or valley, had to be given an understand-able form. It was vital for this energy to be personi- fied into an acceptable humanised form, so as to be able to relate to it. Thus Thor actually became the fierce ambassador of thunder and the storm.

Our Pagan ancestors realised that one could not hope to connect with the whole spectrum of divine creation and influence, by worship/reverence of any one single deity. The diversity of the great energy forces - wind, sky, sun, moon, light, dark etc. were seen as all needing their own respective God/ Goddess. This compartmentalisation of divine power, enabled man to understand and ultimately link with any and all aspects, of divine power - at any and all times of his choosing.

The growth of mythological saga and its increasing complexity, gives us evidence throughout all cultures of deepening social and individual intellect - as intellectual capacity increased, so did the number of deities. Each aspect of the human cycle needed to be expressed and personified by its own God-form, the word 'Idol' links with ideal - meaning the ideal image of perfection in the given sphere being related to at that given time. Deities that originally personified the great forces of nature, took on increasingly complicated roles as their stories show.

The Roman God Mars, had started out depicting the energy force in agricultural affairs (the Romans being farmers long before they became a warrior breed). As society expanded Mars developed into a deity of warfare. He was usually represented as a sturdy young man carrying a torch and spear, the ultimate symbol of masculine valour and chivalry.

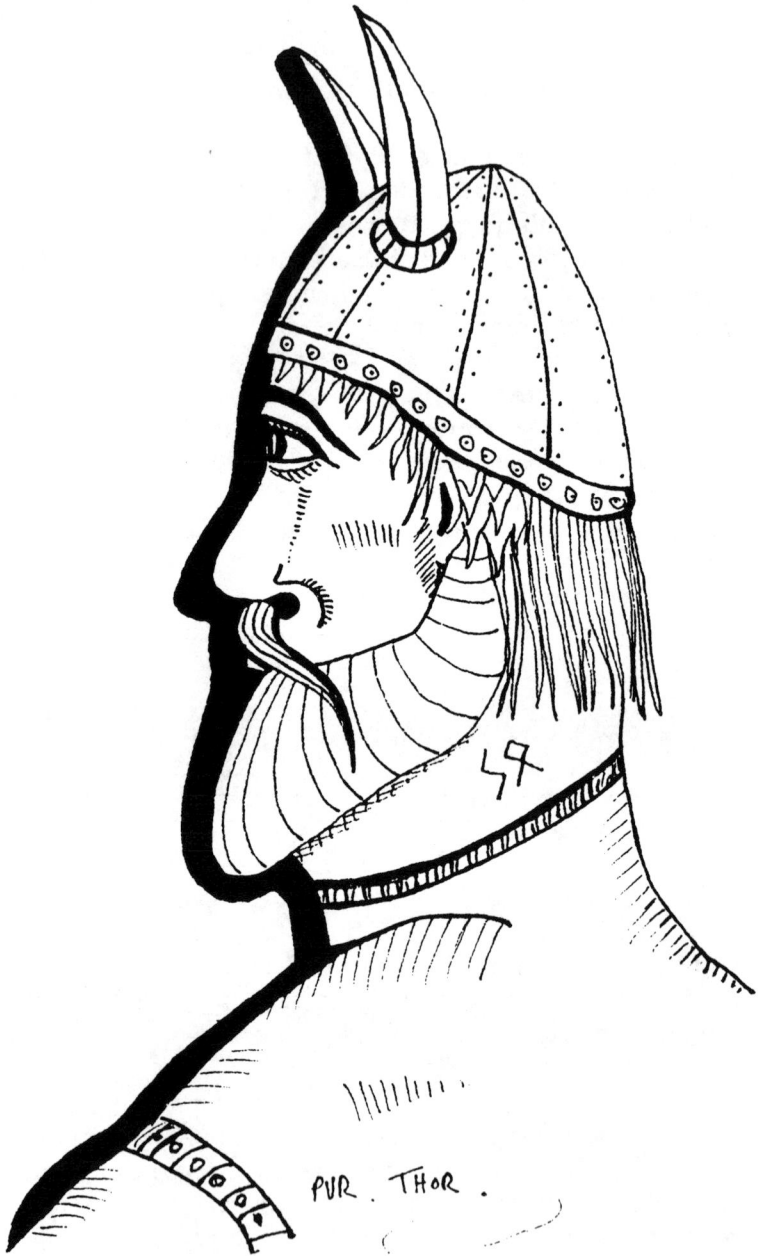

PUR . THOR .

The Salii, priests of Mars performed their ritual dances dressed in complete armour, as a mark of honour to the God. In planetary correspondence Tuesday is given as the day of Mars, and Tuesday itself is named after the Northern God of war Tiw or Tyr. The wolf, horse, and nettle are sacred to Mars, and at first glance it is not always obvious to see why. The wolf is associated with death and battle because of its predatory, carnivorous hunting behaviour wherever one finds him death lies close by. Wolves once roamed the counties of Britain and were vigorously hunted by Briton and Saxon alike; moreover fossilised remains of wolf have been discovered in Pleistocene deposits throughout Europe.

Romulus (mythical founder of Rome) *'Son of Mars'* was suckled by a she wolf along with his twin brother Remus. Romulus and Remus initiated the Lupercalia festival to commemorate their fosterage under a wolf, Canis-Lupus being the contemporary scientific title given to this species. The Lupercalia was celeb rated on 15th Feb and 5th Dec and it was also known as the Faunalia. Both Faunus and Lupercus were Roman equivalents of the Greek God of fertility Pan.

One ancient myth tells us that Faunus/Lupercus is a son of Mars, so it would appear that there is an equation between Romulus and Faunus as they both are depicted as sons of Mars. Moreover their connection with this festival links them at a prime level. The Luperci - priests of Lupercus, would dress up during the festival in Goat skins, then run through the city streets striking out with goatskin thongs at everyone they came across, especially women. This was performed to ensure the blessings of impregnation from the God himself. The Luperci, on a Shamanistic level actually partook of the fertilising energy force of the invoked God form, moreover the believers who participated (often naked), would unwittingly on a subconscious level, place upon themselves the necessary magical mind-set required to ensure pregnancy.

'MARS' - LORD OF WAR.   PVR 45.

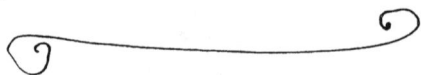

Connections with the wolf and goat remind us of this festival's ancient rural origin, and links with the herdsman and the animals in his charge. Goatskins figured strongly in any rituals involving Pan/Lupercus. He was portrayed as a bearded/horned man with goats legs playing his shepherds pipes. Pan was believed to wait quietly in ambush along lonely country paths for solitary travellers. He would suddenly appear thereby causing the poor individual to flee in terror. The strange primordial fear that one may experience when lost on a cold, deserted mountainside gives us a first hand contact with this God-form's mischievous nature and the meaning of the word *'panic '*.

Mark Anthony is on record as actually performing the role of *'Lupercus'*, showing us how important and popular this feast day once was. Because of its explicitly sexual undertones, the Lupercalia was banned by Pope Gelasius who reigned in AD 492-6, however the public were totally outraged and demanded it's reintroduction. The Pope was forced to comply and later apologised for this act of censorship.

Sexuality has unfortunately been twisted into pornography but ancient cultures celebrated life and sexuality. Phallic symbolism in all and every guise depicted fertility and cosmic energy. A single modern exhibit of a naked man with erect penis, however, caused uproar in a Liverpool gallery. Local fundamentalist organisations grabbed the moral high ground and called for censorship. claiming that they knew what was 'best' for society.

Early man would have at least failed to see what all the fuss was about, or actually regarded such censorious actions as being blasphemy against the Gods. The phallic image gave early cultures hope for new life and growth, the naked human form was something to celebrate, not cover up and lead to shame. Modern therapists know that when sexual opportunity is available at all times and the human body left

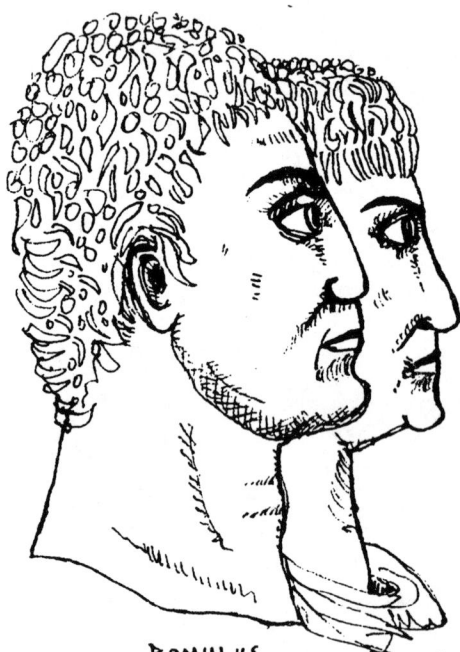

ROMULUS
AND REMUS.   PVR.

uncovered, as in ancient societies (and also modern tribal culture) that one particular thing happens - nothing! It is only when the human form and sexuality are denied, that the problem of sexually repressed behaviour really starts to happen.

Over 1000 years of Christian imprinting and moralising have left the populace of these Isles with a sub-conscious sexual immaturity and guilt complex, that is profitable only to the tabloid press who milk it for all it's worth. Female suppression is of course quite natural to all patriarchal societies ruled by men, God is all powerful to such male dominated cultures. God is male, the father or son image is ingrained deeply into contemporary consciousness. Expressions like 'Oh my God', 'God help me' or 'For God's sake', gush automatically out of Christian and non-Christian mouths alike, usually without the users even being aware that they have been imprinted from birth, by the mind controlling ethos in which they exist.

The Goddess, the great Mother herself was first suppressed then hidden from the masses, leading to much tension and unbalance in modern society, making the female a second class citizen. Evidence is clear of this demotion, when we consider all the hullabaloo caused whenever women have demanded equal rights throughout history. Votes for women campaigners, feminist activists or supporters of women priests, have of course all caused the male dominated mind control caucuses to roll into action, they don't like their monopoly of thought policing to be threatened, and naturally never will. The truth is plain to see, banish the Goddess on higher levels of consciousness, and you reduce the female gender to a lower class of being than man. The Goddess will return and bring balance to mankind for without female divinity the God remains sterile, and so does humanity.

P.V.R.

'THE SHE-WOLF.

The God Mars was associated with the horse many years prior to his role as a powerful state war deity. As a rural God of the woods and fields, he was known as Mars Silvanus. In this role Mars was the personification of the growing force inherent in vegetation. Farmers in ancient Rome would offer sacrifices of fruit, corn and cattle to Mars, hoping that this would lead to abundant crops next year. Modern folk customs like processions featuring *'Green George'* the spirit of vegetation and also to some extent May King/Queen parades owe much of their inheritance to Mars.

On the 14th March in classical Rome, a man clothed in animal skins was chased out from the city streets. The man represented the *'old Mars'*, which as we know mirrors the spirit of vegetation. It was necessary to rid the city of the old decaying force of nature in order for it to be supplanted by the new. Later as Mars became, like society, more sophisticated and warlike, the usage of horses for cavalry increased, and their value in conquest appreciated. The Roman military mind had no difficulty linking the horse's role in combat with the God Mars. The sudden unexpected appearance of a horse, was taken by the Romans to be a sure omen of war or death.

On the 15th October every year a great chariot race took place on the field of Mars, the right-hand horse of the winning team was later sacrificed to Mars, as an offering to ensure good crops during the following Summer. Such base rites are of course repulsive to modern man - however we must remember that in ancient times, virtually all cultures performed sacrifices.

The best of the harvest, flock or race, was offered up as a token especially for the Gods. Man's need took second place. Those who hold the Bible to be the ultimate truth (and use it to attack native Pagan faiths), would do well to realise that The Old Testament particularly Leviticus, is a bloody

VESTA. PVR.

anthology of burnt sacrificial offerings of bullocks, sheep, fowls, turtle doves etc., enough to heartily sicken any person possessing the smallest shred of compassion for the animal kingdom.

The humble nettle was sacred to the God Mars, it's painful sting placing it in association with the realm of war. Nettles are also great survivors, popping up all over the place much to the annoyance of avid gardeners. The Romans, in cold countries like Britain, even used nettles as a type of circulatory stimulant - by stroking themselves with bundles of nettles in order to promote heat. Modern herbal users know well that this wild plant is an excellent blood purifier, it also contains a great deal of iron and is tasty as a cooked vegetable, moreover it produces a lovely full bodied green country wine second to none.

Nature loving gardeners should also remember that nettles are the food plant of many beautiful butterflies and moths, including the Red Admiral and Small Tortoiseshell, so by destroying nettles we also rob these fabulous insects of their much needed nursery grounds. It is easy to reach for the scythe following a nasty sting, however spare a thought for the nettle's good qualities and use a dock leaf instead to ease your discomfort.

The Gods always provide close at hand cure and the dock's antidote to nettle rash is known even to small children, an ancient cultural common wisdom that is literally as old as the hills. Everything in creation eventually has to relate to it's original source which is of a necessity organic and Mars is no exception.

We have seen how this deity started off as a God of nature, it is possible that he may have been occasionally regarded as a solar deity. Mars carried his son Romulus up to heaven in a fiery chariot, which to all intents and purposes must remind

MARS.   PUR.

us of other Gods possessing solar attributes, like the Celtic Lugh or Roman Apollo.

The name Mars may link with the Babylonian deity Marduk, who was also a God of the growing cycles of nature. Marduk, like Mars had solar attributes and was very much a state deity. It is possible too, that Mars gets his name from the root word *'Mar'* - *'to shine'*, if this is evidence of the Roman war God's earlier role being a solar one, then it is possible that he followed a similar pattern of mythological growth to many other Gods.

The attributes of Mars, as we know changed from those connected with agriculture to military activity. He may also have absorbed solar links from earlier deities just like the Celtic Lugh had done. The Sun has and always will be the origin of all organic growth, so it is only natural that Man's earliest attempts to make sense of his own role in the scheme of things, should first include directly or indeed indirectly the solar force itself. The fact that solar energy is the origin of all growth including mankind, is also evident in many deities. Gods like Lugh, Mars, Apollo, Beli, Nodens etc. have shown solar affinities and this is quite normal.

Our ancestors knew that without the all conquering sun nothing was possible. Military conquest was naturally equated with the victory of the sun over darkness, and the Summer's constant battle against Winter. All deities representing any type of victory sooner or later took on solar attributes, sometimes they in fact possessed Sun affinities first, then later as society progressed their earlier solar role was forgotten as another tribe or clan adds on its own particular requirements to the God's depicted image.

The Greek/Roman God Apollo displayed many solar attributes and affinities. He was seen as a God of retributive justice, casting down glittering shafts from his bow and

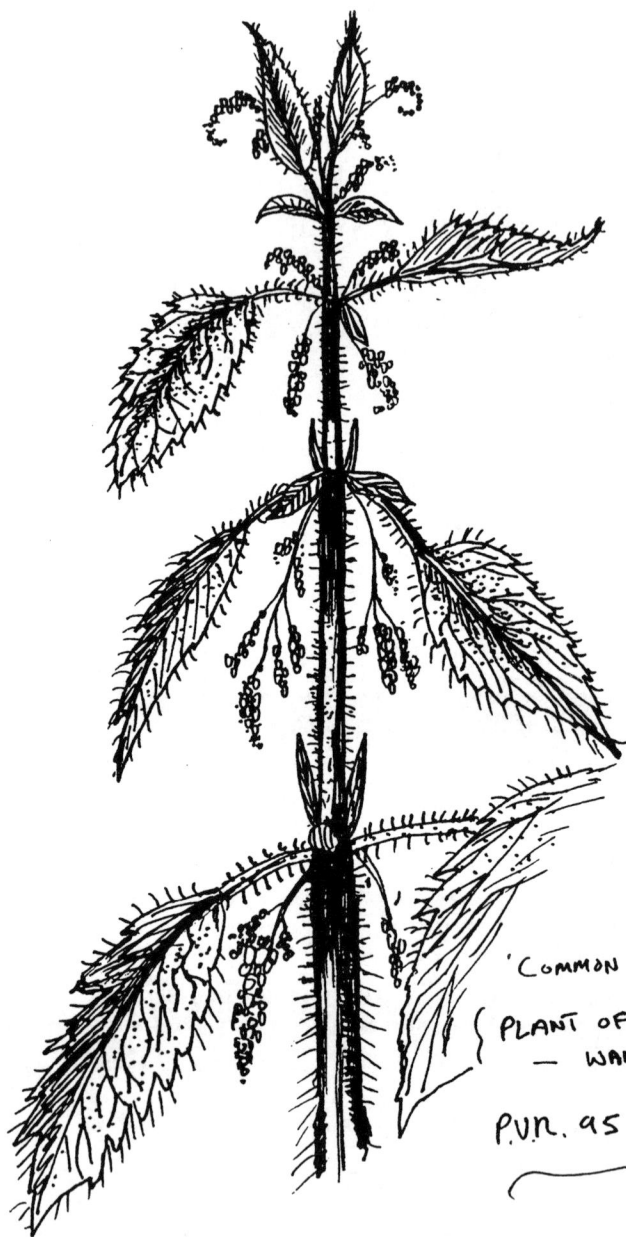

'COMMON NETTLE'.
{ PLANT OF THE
  — WAR GOD }.

P.V.R. 95.

arrows upon insolent law breakers. The place where he was born adorned itself with a *'golden'* robe of lovely flowers, and several critics have regarded Helios the Sun God as actually being the first genuine Apollo, although Homer describes these two deities as being wholly separate and distinct. Apollo could only be approached with a pure loving heart, and a sense of self analysis was required in order to partake in his wondrous mysteries and priestly devotion. He stood for all that was noble, pure and beautiful, one of his most common epitaphs was *'apollo phoebus'* (the pure or bright). His worship came from the Lycians who brought it to Greece, and it was them that first hatched the concept of this type of humanisation of divinity.

Apollo's sacred attributes were the plectrum, snake, bow and quiver, raven, shepherd crook, cithara (non-bowed string instrument), tripod, Laurel, wolf, cock, hawk, grasshopper and Olive tree. This extensive list displays the God's many talents, and also goes some way to explaining why he was often equated by the Romans with the Celtic light God - Lugh, who also had many skills matched to solar attributes. In art and sculpture, Apollo is depicted as a beautiful youth resplendent with flowing hair over his high Forehead. He stands proud with an illustrious intermarriage of pure intellect and physical grace. We may liken him to a maturing *'Lugh'* of superior form and heightened sophistication - in essence the personification of perfected spiritual, intellectual and physical form combined together in man.

The Persian Indian Sun God - Mithras or Mithra was adopted by the Roman legions and he had temples throughout Britain, particularly in the region of the Hadrianic Wall. In the early days of Christianity, worship of Mithras was on a par with that of Christ. During the middle of the 4th century, zealots (probably Christian) desecrated the Mithraeum at Carrawburgh and other temples throughout Britain and Europe. Christianity realised that

Mithraism was a serious contender for the role of state organised religion. Christianity adopted many rites and functions of Mithras worship including the strange head gear of Christian Bishops 'The Mitre', originally a hat worn by priests of Mithras to depict their contractual bonds and approval in religious matters.

The Christian Holy Communion has connections with the earlier Mithraic sacrificial offering of a bull that was slaughtered above the worshipper over a grid, allowing the blood of the beast to flow onto the initiate below.

Legend declared that Mithras slew a bull which represented the chaotic sexual forces inherent in nature and man. By killing the bull Mithras kills the dark uncontrollably negative side of himself. Following this rite the initiate was 'born again' and rejuvenated into a new life. He had symbolically partaken of the 'body and blood' of his God. The significance of this ancient ritual is evident in contemporary Christian worship, the body and blood of the deity however, now being placed in a communion chalice instead of a slaughterers grid-iron trench.

Like Christianity, Mithraism was a patriarchal, masculine orientated faith, and women were excluded from it's mysteries. They worshipped Cybele instead who was a Phrygian fertility Goddess. Mithraism was extremely popular with the military - it's virtues included purity, truth and loyalty. It was introduced into Rome in 68 BC by a collection of Cilician pirates, whom Pompey had captured and whose national religion it was.

Worship of Mithras spread quickly through much of the empire as his dynamic persona appealed to young and old alike. He was usually depicted as a beautiful young man dressed in Phrygian attire with a cap on his head. Incidentally, it is interesting to note that during the

December feast of the *'Saturnalia'* Romans would also frequently wear a little cap, a tradition that is still with us when we wear funny party hats Following the mid-Winter/Xmas dinner.

On ancient mosaics Mithras was usually seen as kneeling astride the bull, thrusting a dagger into its neck surrounded by a Raven, dog, snake, crescent etc - representing the 12 signs of the Zodiac. The similarity of the later figure of Christ at the last supper with his 12 Apostles is no odd coincidence either, Christianity merely changed star signs for disciples.

The number 12 was very significant to aspirants of Mithras for they were required by their betters to perform 12 successive steps or degrees symbolically marked by the names of birds and animals, in order to achieve admittance to the mysteries. Also like the later Christ figure, Mithras was seen as a self-sacrificing deity. By slaying the sun-bull or the materialistic earthly side of himself, he ensured the survival and growth of the spirit/soul after death, which made his worship hugely popular. The word mitra originally meant *'sun'*, however as societies developed it was later given to imply *'contract'* meaning that people could abide together peacefully without resorting to warfare, or internal strife.

Unfortunately human nature being as it is, the positive attributes of this deity were often over-shadowed by the negative. As we have discussed, earlier Sun Gods frequently became Gods of war and Mithras was no exception, as his temples constructed by the Roman military even in Britain prove. The unquenchable desire for political conquest and new lands has throughout history led to persecutions in all cultures.

The popular deity of the day whether it be Mithras, Christ, Lugh, Odin, Mars etc. would be invoked to help in the total

merciless destruction of the enemy. This type of state approved genocide in the name of an often originally *'peaceful'* deity, reminds us of man's inhumanity to man, and his complete failure to appreciate the real inherent spiritual meaning behind his own chosen God-form. Gods are frequently used as a scapegoat to disguise human shortcomings, and following warfare this fact becomes crystal clear, Mars and Mithras being just two small examples.

It is quite possible that if women would have been given access to Mithraism, then it could indeed have developed into a state approved religion of today. It's insistence on moral purity and contractual social development gave the early church of Christ cause for serious worry. Mithraism was the religion of many well-respected, well mannered statesmen, politicians and dignatories, who often led lives of such dignity and grace, that shamed others.

Mithras stood for all that was good, strong, friendly and sociable in human society. Unlike Christianity, Mithraism did not turn the other cheek, it did not suffer fools and was uncompromisingly realistic in its treatment of criminals and other offenders of social standards. In very many ways Mithras is still with us today. Contemporary warmongering so-called Christian politicians would seem to have more virtues in common with Mithras than Christ.

The followers of Mithras realised that moral purity did not entail turning the other cheek. They accepted the natural law that self defence was and had to be, a prime human right for survival of mankind just as in any other species upon the planet. Mithraic adherents may have had their heads in the clouds, but their feet were firmly rooted on the ground. The promise of an afterlife did not make them lose their essential understanding of the materialistic realm in which they dwelt.

Mithras demanded survival of the fittest, loyalty to those who deserved it, and high moral behaviour. In return for these virtues Mithras offered a secure afterlife and sensible guidance in the here and now. Unlike Christianity, Mithraism was tolerant of other deities and faiths, moreover in many temples of Mithras, statues and images of Bacchus, Minerva, Pan, Serapis and other divinities existed side by side with Mithraic reliefs.

This religious system was not then a completely absol- utist form of belief like Christianity. Although male dominated, it recognised other deities and their worthiness. In the best Roman tradition it kept an open mind as to each individual's spiritual right to choose their own particular path of worship. Roman organised thinking was well suited to the worship of Mithras, his promise of social order, moral grace and lack of totalitarianism made sure that his adherence spread far and wide.

The world would have certainly been a very different place today if Christianity had failed in its battle against the 'Lord of light' - Mithras.

Mithras slays the primordial sun bull and new growth and life flows from its veins. This myth is the story of a man giving his all to save humanity, in the truest sense of saviour/martyr terminology. It is a story of a dualistic world view, marking the eternal struggle between light and dark. We have seen that Mithraism did not banish the Goddess. She appears in many Mithraeums, as the statues of Minerva and others prove. Because of this fact Mithraism would have today still undoubtedly respected the male/female, or God/Goddess vital balance in creation. It would, unlike its Christian successor, have given Ies of Cybele their rightful role in the eternal scales of life and justice, oh yes.

Society would play to a very different tune if the old Persian sun God had mastered his biblical rival - Christ. The sacrificial nature of most of the world's religions is evident in Mithraism, and intimately connects to the psychological belief that there can be no life without death, or creation without destruction.

From the earliest times, man had discovered that the raging forest fire eventually created a new habitat for his vegetables and fruit, that the fierce Winter floods brought in massive shoals of edible life giving fish such as Salmon and Sea-Trout and that by forgoing his urge to unearth for food small plants, they would grow on to become a larger crop that he could benefit from later. He saw all around him the concept and actions of life coming out of death, and this he naturally went on, to apply to his religious world view.

The sacrificial nature of Christianity and the concept of a deity dying to save the souls of its followers is by no means a new idea. The Christian Easter Spring celebration owes much of it's origins to the Greek God of the corn and resurrection 'Adonis'. The name Adonis comes to us from the semitic 'Adon' meaning 'Lord'. During the Spring equinox worshippers of this God would lament over his death with great solemnity, then later his revival was joyously celebrated with great feasting and music.

Adonis was adopted in the seventh century before Christ by the Greeks, so his heritage was very ancient indeed. He was originally a Mesopotamian deity called Tammuz, the Greeks misinterpreted his title of Lord Adon thinking it to be his actual name, and this nom de plume remained.

Adonis was depicted as a beautiful youth, who was killed by a wild boar near a river. His injuries caused the river to turn red with blood, and it is quite interesting to note that many rivers after heavy rains, do indeed change to a reddish hue,

SERAPIS

PVR

which is of course due to particles of earth, peat and clay etc, being eroded from the surrounding landscape then washing into the waters.

Myth has it that Adonis, like Persephone - the Greek Corn Goddess, spent half a year in the lower world and half in the upper world. Adonis was lamented over in Bethlehem long before the birth of Christ. Bethlehem means *'House of Bread'*, so it is quite feasible to make a connection between the growth of corn, bread and the deity himself.

The lover of Adonis was the Goddess Venus or Aphrodite, who may in this legend be seen as the great Earth Mother annually lamenting the decay of the spirit of vegetation. Venus by the way, is linked in planetary correspondence to Friday (Freya's-day). Originally a Goddess of Spring growth, Venus later took on many of the attributes of the Greek Love Goddess Aphrodite.

Fish were regarded sacred to all love/fertility Goddesses, because of their link with life giving water and flood myths. Fish were eaten on her special day Friday, a tradition that has been adopted by the Catholic Church. The symbol of the fish is now widely regarded as being a Christian emblem, however many uninformed Christians would probably be appalled if they realised that they were inadvertently sporting one of the oldest Pagan Goddess symbols today.

It is interesting to note here that the celebrations of the death and resurrection Adonis are still held today under another guise in Haxey, Lincolnshire, with the image of the well known spirit of the cornfields *'John Barleycorn'* on Plough Monday - January 6th. The villagers continue this ancient tradition marking the annual Life/death/life cycle, where John Barleycorn becomes the contemporary consort of the former great Earth Mother, although now unfortunately without the mention of the essential Goddess herself. This

old country song further proves John Barleycorn's link with resurrection deities like Adonis.

> There was three men came out of the west,
> Their fortunes for to try,
> And these three men made a solemn vow,
> John Barleycorn should die,
> They ploughed, they sowed,
> They harrowed him in,
> Throwed clods upon his head,
> And these three men made a solemn vow
> John Barleycorn was dead.

> Then they let him lie for a very long time
> Till the rain from heaven did fall,
> Then little Sir John sprung up his head
> And soon amazed them all.
> They let him stand till midsummer
> Till he looked both pale and wan,
> And little Sir John he growed a long beard
> And so became a man.

The song finally tells us that John Barleycorn is cut off at the knee, rolled over, trussed up at the waist, beaten with sticks, stabbed through the heart with a pitchfork, then ground betwixt two stones.

John finally becomes *in the glass* the stronger man at last. Amongst much cheer and merriment the happy Lincolnshire revellers, at this cue raise their beer tankards and nobly salute the females present. It is plain to see here that John Barleycorn represents the masculine fertilising God force, that helps the corn seed to germinate, grow on then become a golden harvest in late Summer. John's death then becomes the cut crop and his rich transformation is marked by the first taste of frothy new beer. The new season heralds his resurrection once again, with the first green shoots slowly inching toward the pale March Sun on cold barren brown fields. Manifold traditions such as John Barleycorn exist worldwide, many are transparently disguised now in Christian clothing. However all intimately relate to the ancient Pagan wisdoms possessed by our early forefathers since the first human drew breath.

A feast day called the Veneralia was annually held in honour of Venus, and April was deemed to be sacred to her. The Spring is a time of bursting buds and beautiful natural growth. Adonis with his resurrection and return to Venus is a lovely classical tale, marking the renewal of nature's abundantly creative life force, that of course also works within us too. Adonis, Christ, Osiris and Mithras all reflect man's desire for salvation. The sacrificial God/King, becomes humanitie's psychological safety net or scapegoat figure that, like the ancient Hebrew goat was burdened to carry off the sins of the people out into the desert. This is the way of the dualistic mindset, philosophies/religions that perceive life on all levels, as being of a black/white or good/ evil nature. They need the scapegoat or martyr figure to depend upon. This takes care of any reluctance or inability of participants, to rectify imbalances in negativity that they prefer to call evil. The personification of evil itself is regarded as a separate force, a force in direct opposition to the sacrificial omnipotent God force that is their salvation.

Sexuality has also been used as a mind control gambit by Christianity for eons. According to rabbinical theology the second wife of Adam - Eve (Lilith being the first), disobeys God and eats the forbidden apple, this event marks the beginning of original sin. This in turn puts believers in a state of disgrace from the day they are born i.e. original sinners. Lilith was to be demoted to the ranks of a demoness - the Temptress, which marked women as second class citizens right from the very start.

Sexual abstinence as displayed by modern Catholic clergy owes much of it's origins to the ancient priests of the God Attis/Atys. Attis was the Phrygian version of Adonis, legend has it that Attis was like many other Gods born of a virgin mother, in this case 'Nanna'. He met his doom by castrating himself and bleed- ing to death under a Pine tree. During the rites of Attis and Cybele/Kybele (his mother/lover), worshippers would, like their God, mutilate themselves, thus as with Catholic clergy celibacy would be enforced on entry into the mysteries.

Such seemingly unnatural occurrences, are explained as a subconscious human desire to express grief at the passing of the God, who in any form represents the waning cycle of nature. In order to achieve full understanding of the deity, worshippers felt that they must suffer the shame, humiliation and pain of a sort of symbolic death, before again (like the God) being reborn into a new life.

The desire to please a deity by acts of abstinence, suffering, penance or celibacy, also links intimately with the concept of self purification. The God again becomes a scapegoat to be used for psychological self cleansing, a mode of symbiotic assistance. By pleasing the God form the worshipper, with his penance, became greater than before, he gave to the God and in turn the God gave to him. The more he gave the more he received, self sacrifice being just another form of deity payment whether performed with love, lust or simply fear.

The concept of a Goddess like Cybele being the mother and also the lover of the God has led to many confusing and misleading statements throughout the ages. This of course is quite understandable if the observer is only capable of viewing the situation through dualistic, black and white eyes. The Pagan spectator on the other hand, knows (or should know) that this son/lover notion must relate to the natural forces inherent in nature. The great Goddess Cybele

was also known as Agdistis or Dindymene, throughout Western Asia she was honoured as *'Mother of the Gods'*. Cybele was adopted by the Greeks who equated her with their earth Goddess *'Rhea'*.

The Romans considered her to be identical to their Goddess *'Ops'*, wife of Saturn, and Roman priests of Cybele were known as Galli. In the land of Phrygia her priests were called the Corybantes, they supervised her rites with loud music played on horns, cymbals and drums.

It is very interesting to note that the Corybantes performed their rituals in full armour, just as the later Roman priests of Ares/Mars had also done. It would be feasible to assume that the Romans did then adopt this tradition of armoured ritual dress from the Mother Goddess of Phrygia and her devotees.

Cybele was often depicted in art or on coinage as being seated in a car pulled by lions, or riding on a lion's back. It may be quite possible that there is some connection here with the Norse Goddess Freya/Frigga who is, as we have discussed, often portrayed driving a chariot drawn by cats. Freya was also referred to as the Mother of the Gods like Cybele, so this strengthens the hypothesis yet further. Worship of Cybele travelled far and wide, she had a following in London where various statues of her have been discovered. A pair of savage looking Roman bronze forceps were also retrieved from the Thames at London Bridge that were believed to have been used by the Galli to castrate initiates, before entry into the mysteries.

Legend has it that the great Goddess fell deeply in love with a young shepherd called Attis, she discovered to her horror and grief that Attis had been disloyal to her, so she drove him insane. Shortly after this he unmanned himself under the Pine tree and bled to death. Attis as a God was resurrected, the Goddess turned his blood to beautiful red flowers to herald his safe return in the Spring. Cybele in this instance is the Earth itself, she gives birth to Attis (her son) who is proudly seen as the increasingly fertile solar aspect of life.

In Summer time Attis becomes her lover, marking the sacred marriage and zenith of nature's growth and fertility. With his death we see the onset of decaying vegetation and Winter's victory over Summer, where Attis takes on the character of dying lover. Cybele then, is like numerous other Mother Goddesses, the feminine nurturing, responsive energy that awaits the return and resurrection of her son/lover, the God/masculine force in nature, necessary to ensure future growth. Explicitly or indeed implicitly the Goddess is always, in pre-Christian religions, seen as recovering the God from his dark realm.

In Winter she, unlike the God, does not die, she merely displays her 'life in death aspect', she becomes the old crone, death Goddess, savage mother or war Goddess. The latter may go some way to explain why the Corybantes dressed in full armour for what was otherwise a religious rite. The vernal equinox being the start of the Summer season, also gives us further evidence of the way in which worshippers perceived Cybele as a fertility/war Goddess.

Attis and Cybele were celebrated during the Spring, particularly in March and April, the time when the Goddess is portrayed as the maiden of regrowth. She is young and eager to raise her son into manhood, a mythological concept that appears in nature as the increasing height of the sun (son), that coincides with the glory of Spring flowers and rich tapestry of early Summer's green.

Attis the God of new life, is impelled to sacrifice his true self at the height of his manhood, in order to bring the Goddess to fruition, which was expressed by the passionate lament of worshippers, for the God's passing young life. This resurrection by the Goddess into new life was celebrated with rapturous joy.

The modern Christian Easter time exclamation of '*he has risen*' would have been commonplace amongst the ancient Phrygian people, long before Christ was ever born. It is not surprising that early Christianity assumed the mythological concept of previously dead and born again Gods into it's own minority cult. Without such an incorporation, Christianity could never have hoped to achieve any meaningful level of popular advocacy.

The early church was impelled to adopt the whole universal nature of Pagan festivities, traditions and holy days and make them it's own. This was primarily because, in order to gain support for it's cause, the church had to give the historical figure of Christ a valid calender of dates and feast days to connect him to the seasonal earthly cycles of the year. Without this the Christian cult would have been totally unable to portray it's founder as a resurrected Messiah. Any serious open-minded individual need not delve very deeply into mythological study to discover that monotheistic, patriarchal faith is built on a vast indigenous Pagan substructure.

It is necessary to fully understand these things, in order to personally make a step forward into the light of mythological enlightenment. It has to be achieved on a personal level first, or else one is merely a leaf drifting in the wind of cultural ignorance. By accepting third hand information we become an easy tool for the mind movers in society to manipulate. This is why many mystics and seers, like the shadowy Merlin figure in Arthurian legend, have always been depicted in a reclusive way.

Incidentally Merlin in Arthurian myth always seems to stand apart from the rest of Arthur's entourage. Some writers have credited him with solar/sky attributes and suggested his earlier worship at Stonehenge etc. as a Sun God under the name of Myrddin or Emrys. His great importance is made very clear in an old name for Britain *'Clas Myddin'* meaning - Myrddins Enclosure, moreover his wife in one myth is called the only daughter of *'Coel'*, who we have previously discussed as being linked to the Celtic War God - Camulos.

If Merlin was then inextricably connected to such a powerful war deity, albeit by family ties then proof of his high esteem must become patently obvious. Rather than only being a simple magician as in later Christianised Norman romance, Merlin was probably originally thought of as a type of Brythonic Zeus or Apollo. It must be mentioned in passing, that there was once a sixth century bard called Myrddin and it is likely that many of the stories of both this personage, and the deity in question overlapped, just as similar tales of the historical and mythological Arthur had done also.

Merlin is featured in a myth concerning the semi-historical King Vortigern of Kent who reigned in the 5th century. Vortigern hired Saxons under Hengist and Horsa, to help him fight against savage Picts and Scots. Many reports of this affair now give conflicting and inconsistent accounts, however the Saxons grew too powerful for their British hosts and soon drove out or enslaved the native populace. Vortigern's mystics persuaded him to build a tower, which unfortunately collapsed, so they told him to use the young blood of a male bastard to cement the unstable foundations (this was obviously intended as a type of sacrificial offering to ensure success) and make them strong.

Merlin was born of a Welsh princess following her intercourse with a demon. From birth the child had shown great powers of prophecy and magic. He was brought before King Vortigern and soon the young mystic had the old King listening to his wisdom with both ears. Vortigern was told that his own seers were fools that would only lead him astray. The King was fascinated to hear that under the tower there existed a pool which prevented the foundations from holding their ground. Vortigern's men dug deeply under the tower and eventually came upon the watery pool just as Merlin had predicted.

Next Merlin instructed the King to have his workers drain the pool, at the bottom of this place you will discover two stones containing in each a dragon that has not yet awoken. Vortigern did as Merlin had commanded and in due course two dragons - one white, one red, were released from their deep slumber. These fearsome beasts proceeded to argue furiously, they represented the warring fractions, the red dragon of the British/Welsh and the white dragon of the Saxons. Vortigern's tower (representing the unstable kingdom of Britain) would not stand, due to his previous invitations toward the Saxon mercenaries (white dragon) that had now begun to lay siege to his kingdom.

Merlin, as we know, always seemed to appear at the oddest of times, always ready to issue dire prophecy and warning to the unwisest of souls. This *'fathering'* by a *'demon'* is most likely a Christianisation of his earlier connection to the otherworld or even *'under-sea'* parentage, (similar in fashion to the Celtic God Lugh, whose grandfather Balor was an ugly demonic Fomorian giant). Lugh possessed solar attributes and so indeed did Merlin, as the next examples will show.

Diodorus Siculus was a great historian who was born at Agyrium in Sicily he existed in the same era as Julius Caesar and Augustus, for a long time Diodorus lived in Rome collecting materials for his great work on the history of the world, from the creation to the Gallic wars of Julius Caesar.

PUR 95. STONEHENGE

This epic work was called - *'bibliotheke historike'* and consisted of 40 books that took 30 years to produce.

Diodorus mentioned a *'temple of Apollo'* in Britain that was a *'circular'* enclosure (Myrddin's enclosure ?) in the centre of Britain, obviously relating to Stonehenge.

The worship of Myrddin at Stonehenge was suggested by Professor Rhys, moreover Geoffrey of Monmouth claimed that the stones were erected by Merlin, after being first brought over from the hill of uisnech in Ireland, a place linked closely to *'Balor'* - Lugh's grandfather. Such interconnections with solar/sky deity worship from manifold sources throughout history, show us the true worth of Merlin - not as a crafty sage but an *'all important'* British God, a God that dwells closely in the undercurrent of indigenous Celtic consciousness, waiting so very patiently for the rebirth that is, like the Summer's Sun - long since due.

The solitary seeker of wisdom will no doubt make some mistakes, however he or she will eventually learn vital lessons about life and mythological truth denied to the flock, and it's safety in numbers mentality. Right through the mediaeval years, country people in need of medical or spiritual assistance, would seek out the services of the village wise man or woman, who often as not would live alone in some isolated area. Of course these solitary people held vast native cunning and knowledge, which unfortunately made them easy targets for the Witch hunters who sought victims, to support their cruel work for God.

Living away from common society whether in a physical or spiritual manner also resulted in the church authorities viewing them with suspicion. They, because of their solitude became difficult to control/manipulate, so naturally as with all minorities they were first to succumb to religious intolerance. In all cultures it is always the smallest group or individual that gets it in the neck (sometimes literally) when society needs a scapegoat on which to vent it's wrath. The solitary path can be extremely hard and lonely for some, yet the benefits of real enlightenment make it all worth while in the end.

The solitary seeker of wisdom must in many ways take on a self sacrificing role, he/she is by choosing the solo path, bound to lose a part of his/her old self. This is a type of spiritual metamorphosis, similar to the caterpillars transformation into a butterfly. The birth, death and resurrection cycle of the sacrificial old Gods, also closely connects with this deeply moving aspect of human progressions.

We have previously discussed at some length mythological inter-relationships, that co-exist closely between stories and legends and the seasonal forces of nature. The shedding of the old self and movement towards personal spiritual enlightenment is an exciting step that the ancients cleverly incorporated into mythological innovation.

The story of the Norse God Odin/Woden and the Well of Mimir, is a tale of self sacrifice, spiritual initiation and the quest for greater wisdom. Odin gained the great knowledge for which he is famous for, by visiting the sacred spring of Mimir (memory). He asked for the favour of being allowed a drink from the magical waters of enlightenment and was told that he must exchange one of his eyes before receiving the gift from Mimir. Odin gladly agreed to this request, and thereby gained the knowledge and insight which he so greatly sought.

However Odin's new wisdom did not prove to be completely conducive to absolute happiness, for his new found power also gave him insight into future events that of course were not all beneficent ones. His possible association with the

Grim (Grimr) Reaper, links closely with this story because the true ephemeral nature of cosmic and earthly events, is always marked by the totality of death. Odin in this tale obviously saw the impending doom of the Nordic Gods at the 'Ragnorak'.

This story is told in the *Prose Edda*, and is assumed to have been a prophecy. But it would appear to be more of a distant genetic folk memory of an awesome natural catastrophe, possibly from the Ice Age. Although it must be remembered that the Twilight of the Gods as depicted in the Ragnorak may possibly have picked up many Christian apocalyptic associations, so we often need to view the Ragnorak with a scrutinising eye !

Many writers have remarked on Odin's single eye being emblematic of solar energy (the Sun) and this may be so, however it is also symbolic on deeper human levels as a key to divine truth. The giving of an eye, for an eye of wisdom tells us that at certain times in life, we will and should be prepared to make our own self sacrifices for ourselves and others. In order to receive, we have to be first ready to give; the farmer must be prepared to labour in the field if he wants to reap a rich harvest, the fisherman must endure the cold Winter's storm in order to benefit by a full net, and the artist must spend long hours with brush and paint before the masterpiece is complete.

Odin's sacrifice is given as a gift for mankind to learn from. His suspension for nine days and nights on Yggdrasil is also a gift to us. Odin is the personification of not only wisdom, but also of the spirit of giving to those in need, hence his title *'All Father'*. The modern Father Christmas figure was transparently moulded from Odin/Woden, who rode the night sky on a white horse not a reindeer. The red uniform of father Xmas is symbolic of rebirth as the colour connects with Holly berries.

ODIN.
PUR.

The Holly itself links with modern Xmas festivity because it was used by the Romans during their ancient feast of the Saturnalia, that took place in late December. The Saturnalia gave many of its customs to the modern Xmas celebration. The spirit of giving was expressed by the strange tradition of masters serving slaves as a mark of charity and giving. Incidentally, the custom still survives as officers serving their men in the modern Army during the Xmas meals. This feast was of course sacred to Saturn - Roman God of the crops.

In the temple of Saturn a great banquet was given in which all citizens were invited. After the feasting (as we have previously discussed) every participant would put on a soft cap made of felt called the Pileus. The custom would no doubt have been adopted by the Romans from earlier cultures, possibly Phrygian as the cap was often associated with the Sun God Mithras. It is quite feasible that the cap was used (like the Mitre) by the priests/worshippers of this deity at times of festivity, initiation, celebration or other various rites.

Children received earthenware dolls (Sigilla) and garish pictures from their parents, which is the latter day equivalent of today's youngsters being given computer games, videos and the latest compact discs. Holly sprigs were given to friends and relatives with love, as a token of goodwill, health and happiness; red Holly berries being emblematic of life in death, and sacred to Saturn himself. Wreaths of Holly were hung over doorways as a defence against malevolent spirits and attacks from enemies. Moreover, the spikey foliage of this tree magically linked with defensive weaponry such as the sword, arrow and spear.

The Saturnalia originally took part on only one day-19th December, however Julius Caesar's reformation of the calender caused the date of the feast to be held on the 17th, which of course resulted in much misunderstanding and

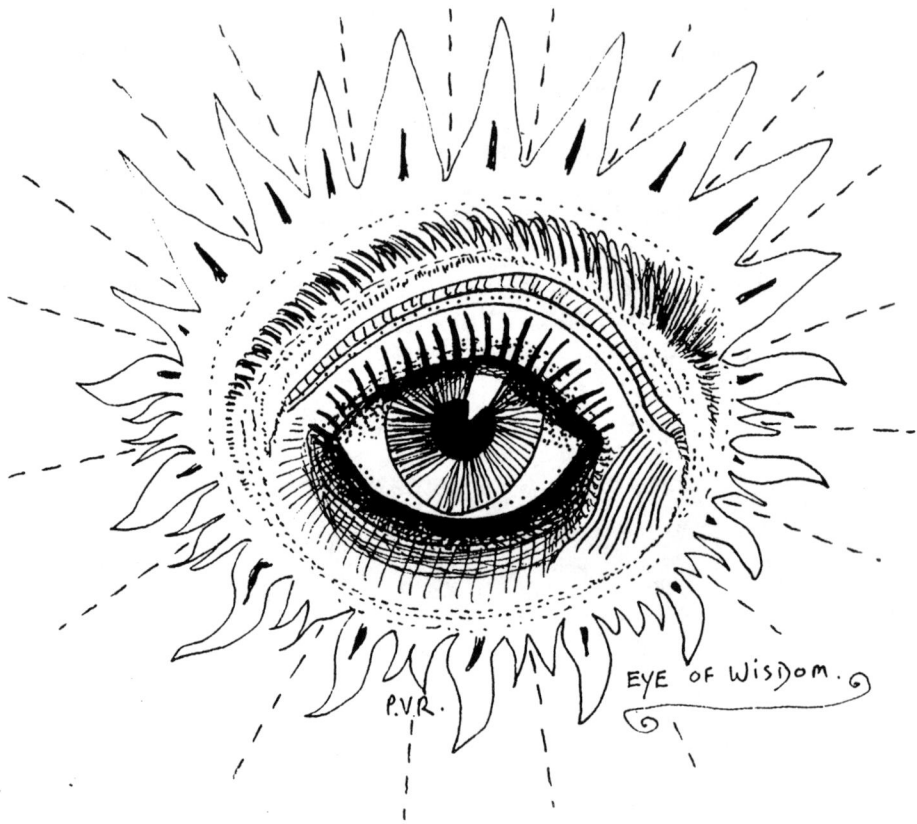

P.V.R.

EYE OF WISDOM.

confusion. The Emperor Augustus later simplified things by declaring that the feast be extended to three days - 17th, 18th and 19th December. Eventually the celebration embraced seven days, as it was a time of great merriment and love. Two other festivals were incorporated into the Saturnalia revelries, first the Sigillaria when the earthenware figures 'Sigilla' were given to children, secondly was the Opalia in honour of Ops, wife of Saturn.

During the celebrations, all business was put on hold, Law court and schools were closed, even military activity was suspended for the week - the mood was one of complete relaxation, joy and sharing. Just like the modern Christmas, merriment could get very noisy with revellers singing and dancing in the city streets.

Those who complain about the mid-Winter feast being too materialistic, had their ancient counterparts in the Saturnalia. The Roman statesman and philosopher 'Seneca' wanted to be left in peace to his meditations, while the young Pliny (also a statesman) actually constructed a sound proof room to escape the rowdy behaviour of the happy throng. Saturn was personified as the Lord of Misrule during this festival, and it is interesting to note that many Hallowe'en customs also contain elements of such a figure, causing havoc and general disorder. This is no coincidence, namely because the incoming Winter season whether celebrated in Italy or in Britain, was regarded by the ancient Pagan cultures as a time of misrule.

They realised that Summer was now over and that soon nature itself would be entering a state of decay and gloom. Saturnalian festivals were an excellent way to relate to the changing natural cycles of life, a time to give joy, friendship and goodwill to family and friends alike.

All over Europe people would dress up as the Lord of Misrule, Bishop of Fools or other similar characters to depict the demise of natural growth. Much of the prankish behaviour has rubbed off on contemporary Hallowe'en festivities. The ancient Celtic people, long before Roman invasion, marked the 31st October Hallowe'en/Samhain as the start of their Winter/end of Summer season. The time when games and merriment would commence. Without doubt the link between Samhain and mid-Winter feasting traditions/customs must owe a great deal to later Roman influences. Samhain was taken by the Celts to be the last chance to let off steam before the cold, gloomy nights of Winter set in.

Roman invasion obviously brought with it the Saturnalian tradition, which somewhere along the line conjoined or merged with traditional Celtic mad-cap celebrations of the oncoming Winter's season. The Lord of Misrule was once probably in pre-historic times an actual person, who as a convicted criminal/ prisoner of war would be given the role of King of Fools or Thieves, and as such became a sacrificial offering or scapegoat symbol used to ensure success with next years harvest.

The depiction of Jesus Christ as King of Jews and his ordeal and death, the crown of thorns and mockery by the soldiers, all point to the not always obvious conclusion that he was regarded then in society as a *'Saturnalian representative'* , who was to take out, like many scapegoat figures before him, the old dying year, in order to let in the new. Because of this we can see that Christ, can give us a deeper in-sight into our true pre-Christian heritage, that is our birth right.

The modern New Year custom of a tall, dark man letting in the New Year, is a relic also of these ancient traditions. Today's Hogmannay feast being the end of the old year was once long ago celebrated at the end of October, which gives us the calender connection with Samhain activities. Many strange parades and processions once took place at this time of year.

One particular curious folk custom in Scotland, involved a man dressing up in a cow skin robe. He would then be escorted by a crowd of many young people to each house in the village, and then he would quickly run three times clockwise (sunwise) around the house, whilst the jolly participants preceded to beat him and the walls of the house playfully with their whipping rods. Eventually the owner would invite one or several of the crowd inside, at which point a blessing for health, happiness and prosperity would be bestowed upon the occupier.

This and many other similar old customs bear a striking resemblance to rites performed by the priests of Pan during the Lupercalia to ensure fertility. The man wearing the animal skin, beating with sticks and the magical raising of creative fertilising energy with the Sun invoking custom, all connect such folk rites to much older Pagan ritualism. First beginnings of the year have always attracted mixed feeling of exciting anticipation, heady exhilaration and of course a hint of sad sentimentality for beloved lost friends and family long since gone. The Celtic people had a special reverence for beginnings and ends of all things. The line of the shore where Sea met land, the start of the Summer, the sacred space above a steed's head, and the first sight of the beautiful rising August Moon, all were seen as holding magical awe.

The start of events was believed by the Roman peoples to be supremely important, and they would ponder over how to tackle any issue, whether military, civil or merely social for a long period, before deciding on the appropriate course of action. In the temples, priests would invoke the assistance of various relevant deities. The entrails of sacrificed animals would be carefully examined for signs and omens. Cloud formations, weather conditions and also flight patterns of birds, would all help them to make a firm decision.

With regards to birds as a method of divination, there is a great deal of logic in this. Their behavioural patterns would have proved vital to the Roman legions intending to embark upon naval activity, as study of bird flight did and of course still does when observed closely, foretell the coming of fine or indeed foul weather. The old maxim 'one Swallow does not make a Summer' holds as true today as it always did. The wise old fly fisherman hoping for a Trout, will always outfish his peers by seeking out the Swifts, Swallows and House Martins that deftly swoop down upon the hatching river flies on the rippling water's surface. He knows that fish will congregate there to feed on the insects too.

The rather gruesome examination of animal viscera for divination purposes, probably had its foundation in materialistic realms. The ancient Roman farmers would no doubt have come to learn, that if the entrails of an animal were bloated, distended or diseased, then famine for the clan was a distinct possibility.

Following this discovery, appropriate steps could have been taken to weed out other weak sickly animals before contamination spread. On the other hand if the study revealed healthy organs, then it could be assumed that the people would not want for food later in the season. Obviously these old truisms, eventually absorbed (through priestly hierarchies) an increasingly mystical purpose and meaning that of course gave greater control to the parties involved, even though the origins of these rites once belonged to a much older Pagan 'common sense' wisdom of life's varying cycles. The Romans believed that everything and its action, had its own particular corresponding spirit or deity.

JANUS P.VR.

Any beginning or starting process was sacred to the God *'Janus'*, and his special place in the scheme of things was to guard doors, gateways and openings. The first month of the year January is named after him, as is the word Janitor because Janus was often represented holding keys. Many writers have mistakenly credited this God with no more importance than being a spirit of doorways. His later function as a deity of gates/doors etc. is quite correct, however his original worship was of a much more special nature. His popular depiction is one of a seated two headed/faced man, one face being that of a youth, while the other (facing in the opposite direction) is that of an old man. In his left hand is a key, the other holds a sceptre. Some authorities have linked Janus with the great Goddess of the Moon and fertility *'Diana'*, making her the divine consort of Janus under the title of Jana.

There also seems to be further evidence of this connection, when we look more closely at the symbolic two faced image of the God Janus. That ancient lunar emblem of the waxing, full and waning Moon's cycle with the two quarters facing in opposite directions, is in fact amazingly similar to the two faced depiction of the classical Janus. He was often given precedence over other Gods even the great Jupiter, and in times of war the temple of Janus had its gates left open. The Roman military machine was so ruthlessly efficient that the gates of Janus were often as not left wide open, the gates when closed became the ultimate symbol of peace and harmony.

Like Jupiter, Janus was frequently referred to as *'Father'*, giving us further proof to his much greater importance than merely being just a lowly gatekeeper. It is quite feasible that these two deities like many others before, were once actually the same God, later becoming (due to tribal dialectal differences) perceived as separate Gods in their own right. A God of gates/openings has to be one of *'supreme importance'* in his

JANUS PUR.

144

current social ethos, as such Janus was a God of beginning, end and rebirth in the natural cycle of cosmic events, including man's universal struggle to understand his/her place in the chaotic nature of world events. Janus held the key to the realms of all mysteries, because he began events and also ended them.

Janus with his two heads depicts the unification of all opposites into a completed whole. In him, past and future combine to take on form in the solidified present zone of time. Janus represents great wisdom and knowing, because he cannot be approached without prior warning. His gaze by viewing what has been and what is to come allows him to be the master of all he surveys. Janus holds in his fist the 'key' to life, and also its hidden mysteries beyond. When one stumbles across the key of Janus it is but one step towards a realisation of the full treasure that lies deeply embedded within his grasp. Such incredibly complex patterns of religious/philosophical thoughts like those held by Janus, show us how very advanced our ancient ancestors really were. Modern man could certainly learn a great deal regarding his/her true self by returning to the worship and understanding of pantheons of old Gods, especially the Roman.

In Heraldic symbolism the 'double headed' Eagle relates to the earlier image of Janus. Many countries have sported this lofty emblem of power throughout world history. As suggested above Janus and Jupiter may have once, originally been one and the same deity. This hypothesis is strengthened further when we examine the Eagle's interconnection with Janus, and also Jupiter. In Romano/Greek art and sculpture the Eagle was depicted as Jupiter/Zeus' bird, (Zeus of course being the original Greek prototype of the Roman Jupiter). This magnificent bird soaring beyond the vision of the human eye, was believed to benefit by it's approach to the Sky God, so naturally it became his own sacred symbol.

PVR. 'ZEUS'

One legend sees Zeus being brought a thunderbolt by the Eagle as he prepared to do battle with the Titans, moreover this bird holds the bolts of Zeus in his powerful talons, providing courage and inspiration to heroes of old. We know of Janus' epitaph as a spirit of beginnings, the Eagle too may be seen as depicting in subconscious emblemism,the dawning of the transcendent odyssey of the human soul/spirit toward the light of supreme divinity. The bronze and silver standards proudly held high by the victorious Roman legions, featured the images of an Eagle with wings outstretched. This tradition continued into the Napoleonic wars after 1804, when Bonaparte's French troops sported gilded Eagles instead of the previous banners.

The mystical symbolism of the colours red combined with white, seen in the Celtic red eared white hounds of Annwn, and the quarrelling red/white dragons of the King Vortigern legend, also appears in the symbolic depiction of Eagles. A 'white' crowned Eagle in a 'red' field was once the shield of the Kingdom of Poland. Red with white seems in fact to link with aspects of immortality, divinity and rebirth. Magnificent qualities such as these would then help us to understand the interconnection between the proud majestic Eagle climbing high toward the Sun, and supreme deities like Jupiter and Janus.

If the Eagle represents the flame of light, sunset and life's positive aspects, then its exact opposite in emblematic idealism is depicted in that sinister creature of the night - the Owl. We have previously discussed the story of the Welsh God of light, Llew, his transformation into an Eagle and the misplaced trust in Blodeuwedd who finally becomes cast out into the form of an Owl. Mythological stories such as this, hinge on the positive and negative aspects of humanity, divinity and nature's changing face throughout the seasons. Each specific aspect being essential to the balance of the other. Winter cannot exist without the following Summer,

HECATE IN HER TRIPLE ASPECT.

conversely the Eagle is balanced with the Owl which is a darker *'other half'*.

The Owl was sacred to many deities and because of it's large *'all seeing'* eyes of wisdom, the ancients gave it pride of place with Athene, Minerva, Hecate and the Greek Goddess of the underworld - Persephone, (known to the Romans as *'Proserpina'*). The Owl's connection to the dead of night links then inextricably to the *'lower-world'*, realm of death and also the Moon. Their mystery makes them birds of divination (the wise one) and the dark/hag aspect of the eternal Goddess. Hecate was often represented in Greek/Roman sculpture as being of *'three-fold'* appearance, three Goddesses in one. This of course refers to her guise as the cycle of womankind, maiden, mother and crone, and also her link as a Thracian lunar deity to the mysterious three phases of the (waning, full and waxing) Moon.

Hecate had, at her command all the wild nocturnal powers of nature. Her triple aspect again comes to the fore, when we find that birth, life and death were also credited to her great list of talents. Hecate's festivals were usually held at night when the Moon was in evidence, worshippers would gather by torchlight. These mysterious events frequently took place at crossroads. This was because these places depicted the four quarters of the lunar orbit. Cakes, buns and loaves with the image of a cross were eaten in celebration at the feast, which probably links to the modern Christian tradition of *'hot cross buns'* on Good Friday.

Hecate because of her sinister associations, was sometimes portrayed with a pack of ravenous underworld hounds, haunting wild places and graveyards. In fact she may possibly be envisaged as a type of ' mistress of the wild hunt ' or feminine *'Herne the Hunter'*, leading the nocturnal entourage through dark places and lonely crossroads at midnight. Her solitary path that follows the nightly flight of

CERES / DEMETER.

PVR. 95.

the Owl, Cat and Nightjar, is remnant of the mystics consciously undertaken journey into the essential unconscious realm of dreams, where all mysteries converge to become tomorrows new enlightened realisations. Hecate then, is a deity of the more shadowy and hidden corners of instinctual feminine wisdom. Persephone on the other hand, while also being a Goddess of the Underworld, appears to have a somewhat gentler, more altruistic type of countenance as the following example will reveal.

Persephone's mother was called Demeter, which probably meant *'Earth mother'*. The Romans knew Demeter as *'Ceres'* which gives us the root of the word 'cereal' from the corn. One bright day Persephone while out picking flowers is abducted by the God Pluto, who carries her off to the Underworld. Her mother - Demeter, searches aimlessly for Persephone and her inability to find her causes the corn to stop growing, making famine fall upon the Earth.

The great God - Zeus intervenes in the crisis, by sending Hermes to escort Persephone back from the Underworld. Pluto, in the heat of the moment slips several pomegranate seeds into Persephone's mouth making her marriage tie to him eternal. The pomegranate has since ancient times been regarded as a symbol of fecundity and oneness of the Universe, moreover the Greeks believed that this fruit grew from the life-blood of Dionysus.

The magical significance is apparent. The manifold seeds inherent in the fruit are emblematic of the great unity that exists throughout life's undulating pattern of events. Zeus has to again intervene, he decides that Persephone should spend half the year with Pluto and the other half with Demeter. This ancient myth gives us a deep understanding of the natural Earth orientated religious wisdom of the pre-Christian races. Demeter portrays the ripe corn which was previously seen in the role of Persephone. Zeus takes on the part of the fertilising rain aspect, and Pluto is naturally the Earth that holds Persephone until she is called back into the light again by Zeus.

The corn maiden and her mother featured strongly in the antediluvian rites called the Eleusian mysteries, which took place in Spring and Autumn throughout the classical world. The lesser Eleusian mysteries were celebrated at the beginning of February and marked the safe return of Persephone from the Underworld to her waiting mother Demeter. This three day rite of Spring renewal obviously gives many of its cultural practices to the modern Pagan celebration of Imbolg, also known as Candlemass or Feast of Lights.

The glimmer of the first pale light of Spring Sun, would be depicted during the mysteries by flickering candles lit at mid- night. The corn maiden was associated with the land of death (Pluto/Hades), so naturally these ancient feasts would be undertaken at the dead of night giving these an even more mysterious air. The greater Eleusian ceremonies went on over a period of nine days and involved processions, music and offerings to the deities involved.

In the time of Herodotus - *'father of history'* (the famous Greek writer born between 490 and 480BC, at the Greek colony of Halicarnassus), it was reported that 30,000 people attended the mysteries. However between 480-430BC, the period of Athens' greatest power, the numbers present would most certainly have been very much higher. These organised events gave the spectator the opportunity to partake in the very mystery of the deity's birth, suffering,death and resurrection, and its symbolic interconnection with the numerous changing cycles of nature.

Persephone is frequently portrayed as holding a pomegranate, (immortality) in one hand, while her other hand clasps a blazing torch (enlightenment). Meditation on the significance of this image alone says more than can possibly be explained in a thousand books, inherent truths and wisdoms condensed by the ancients for us into one concise approachable whole.

Athene/Athena is in her triple guise a Goddess of peace,warfare and wisdom. She was the protectress of Athens, and in Italy the Romans identified her with Minerva the indigenous Goddess of wise council. Athene along with Zeus and Apollo forms the supreme triad in Greek mythology, her origin has several different accounts most likely through variations existing from one place or clan to another. She was believed to have been born from the *'head'* of Zeus fully armed, Zeus felt pains in his head after swallowing his first wife - Metis (wisdom) who subsequently bore the infant.

Because of her parents who represented wisdom and power Athene took on many different attributes. She was deemed to be patroness of arts, law, poetry, agriculture and feminine employment. In her darker role she becomes the Goddess of Battle and storms. She blends harmoniously both the beautiful and the terrible. Her many epitaphs portray this diversely further. They are *'nike'* the victorious, *'hippia'* horse tamer, *'Polias'* patron protectress of cities, *'Ergane'* mistress in industrial affairs, *'Soteira'* the saviour and *'Parthenos'* the virgin Goddess.

The story of her springing out of Zeus' head, may seem rather strange at first appearance. However it contains grains of hidden truth. Zeus was a God of the sky and thunder, which on a deeper level of thought may be analogous with the human subconscious. When he swallows his wife who depicts wisdom, the result is Athene who may be likened to divine inspiration. This equation then gives us the resultant analogy. Zeus is the storehouse of power (the human subconscious). He absorbs Metis (wisdom) and out of his head springs the sum total of this cosmic manifestation, which is Athene.

The divine virgin child portrays genius, intellect and the infinite magical spark of life that subsists throughout the universe. This vestige of mythological enlightenment can be seen with crystalline clarity in the natural world that surrounds us. The sultry August afternoon and its increasing humidity, frequently heralds the coming of ominous thunder clouds leading to a furious blast of lightening splitting the old wizened Oak tree in two. Destructive energy forces no doubt, yet soon the squirrel, wren, owl and woodpecker will seek out in this fresh place future homes to once again create new life.

In the Erechtheum in Athens, there stood a very old figure of Athene, moreover the city contained another image of her that was believed to have fallen out of the wild blue sky. This belief obviously has it's origins in the legend of the Goddess being born of the Sky/Thunder God, and was handed down to the classical Greeks from time immemorial.

The old Druidic practice of building dwelling places from the wood of a previously lightening struck Oak tree, gives us a clue to the old maxim; lightening never strikes the same place twice! (To make a home with such material was deemed to be a protection against thunderbolts and storms). The belief that places blasted by a lightening strike were sacred to the Sky God, may possibly have had it's origins in the pantheons of Greece with particular emphasise on the supreme deity, Zeus.

At Olympia Zeus was venerated under the titles of Thunderbolt and Descender, moreover the Roman counterpart of this God - Jupiter had parallels with similar thunder Gods across Europe and elsewhere. The Nordic people of course knew him as *'Thor'*, to the Teutonic race he was *'Donar'* (Thunder God), to the Slavs he was *'Perunu'*, and the Anglo-Saxons called him *'Thunar'*. The Gauls and Brythonic peoples called him *'Taranis'/ 'Teutates'* ; Taranis meaning the Thunderer, Taranis had shrines stretching from Germany to Britain and it is interesting to note that Taran is still the word used for thunder in Breton and Welsh.

The Nordic Thor was frequently depicted as doing combat with the fierce Frost Giants using his mighty hammer (Mjolnir) to slay them. Incidentally this myth seems likely to relate to the period in early Spring when the ice of Winter begins to melt away, giving us a definitive mythological analogy with this perpetual seasonal change i.e. *'the thaw'* and Thor's victory over the forces of Winter. Today's Christian baptism participants probably do not realise that they owe a lot to Thor, when it comes to their contemporary customs surrounding this old event.

In Scandinavia, babies would be dedicated to the Thunder God with a blessing of water, then the worshippers would make the *'sign'* of Thor's hammer over the infant as a pledge of loyalty to the deity, and to invoke his aid in raising the babe into full healthy maturity. Thor's hammer was held in very high esteem, the Norsemen chiselled it on their gravestones, sacred shrines and dwelling places. It was used during handfasting/wedding ceremonies as a symbol of betrothal and fertility, in the belief that the God would bless the marriage and bring forth children.

Thor, as we have seen earlier was sometimes equated to the Slavonic deity of thunder - Perunu which means to strike or splinter. It is very interesting to note that the name Perunu/Perune may possibly be linked to the Greek word for thunder *'Keraunos'* which sounds very much like the contemporary title of the Celtic horned God *' Cernunnos '*. If this is true then it is likely that Cernunnos, rather than being just a horned God of nature and the woods, may originally have been like Thor, Taranis or Perunu a powerful God of Thunder. The words Keraunos and Cernunnos are phonically speaking very similar, however other similarities between these two deities exist.

The horned God of Nature - Cernunnos was of course widely venerated in Celtic Europe and Britain, many groves and townsteads where he was popularly worshipped contained large forests of mighty Oak trees. This tree has always been sacred to Thunder Gods like Thor/ Donar, so possibly the horned God was honoured here too as a Sky/Thunderbolt deity. The Romans equated Taranis with their God - Dis Pater who was (like Cernunnos) also a Lord of the Underworld.

The famous hill figure known as the Cerne Abbas Giant in Dorset depicts a deity armed with an Oak leaf shaped club. Although this image does not possess horns or antlers, many writers have suggested that he may be a portrayal of Cernunnos. The associations that surround him involving fertility and his oaken club may also be linked to thunder associations, in fact it could be a parallel weapon with Thor's sacred hammer.

It seems quite feasible as often happens in the chronicalisations of ancient myth, that the Lord of the Wild Hunt, fertility and the realm of death becomes cross-linked with the mighty thunder God. We must also think closely about the situation of figures, such as the Cerne Abbas Giant. It may be suggested that such images were carved high upon hill sides to venerate solar power and growth, however where better a place is there to conjoin with the elemental force of the thunderstorm, than these green highly majestic sites of natural grace and beauty ?

The intertwinement between thunder and fertility concepts is increased further still, when we examine the Norse God

Thor's myth. He first married a *'giantess'* called Iarnsaxa (Iron Stone), which again gives us an analogy with the Celtic pantheon where the light Gods were often related to the sinister Giant Fomorians. She bore him two sons - Magni (strength) and Modi (courage).

Thor's second wife was called Sif, unlike Iarnsaxa she was a beautiful (fertility) Goddess with long golden hair. She gave Thor two children called - Lorride and Thrud. His daughter Thrud, was like Thor's first wife - a giantess, who was respected widely for her great size and power. The list of divine combinations where a giant and a God or conversely a Goddess and a giant, conjoin is endless. Sometimes along the great line of mythological change, one deity (as was previously discussed with solar/light/ war gods) inherits attributes that lead to much confusion. Was he/she a Sun, Thunder, Sea, Earth, Hunting God/Goddess or not ? The questions will always pose more and deeper answers.

It is good to ask, for without questions, blind faith will always lead to the destructive path of intolerance and extremism. The word *'why'* is the most potent weapon ever to pass from the lips of man. Mythological works in all cultures must never be taken only at face value, for to accept without analysis is to prevent humanity ever achieving it's full potential, in all levels of existence.

Pre-Christian Pagan mythology was in the past regarded as only being worthy of academic study. It was placed in the cosy coffee club safety of world historical events to be examined with a limited analytically logical mind-set. It was deemed to be unworthy of actual practice, spiritually dangerous or at least vastly inferior to contemporary religious belief systems like Christianity. Modern man with his high tech, high pollution and high stress life style, has for far too long vilified, misunderstood and generally ignored the ways of the old Gods.

Ancient Pagan religions all relate to the natural balance that exists between man and his/her environment. They stand as a means to spiritual enlightenment, and as a path to our personal understanding of how and why we co-exist with other living creatures upon this planet. Fortunately many seekers are now once again learning to appreciate the fabulous gifts of wisdom and joy, that a return to the religions of our pre-Christian forefathers can provide. Deep study of Pagan myth and legend is a powerful key to unlock the doors to self knowledge, moreover it provides a vital escape route to combat the contemporary mind manipulation process that unfortunately affects us all in different ways.

A return to essential Pagan balance and respect for the natural environment is not only desirable, it is absolutely imperative. Global warming, land and sea pollution, rain forest destruction - all these modern horrors and more stand like a rotting epitaph to man's inability to relate to the Earth and all her beautiful green energy flows. Mankind's failure to live in harmony with the planet and understand its many changing moods, has led to the rape of Mother Earth herself. This will not be tolerated by the Goddess, as we always reap what we sow. Modern society. It will, with its unbalanced world view, bring about its own destruction. The healing of our organic home, Mother Earth, has to start on an (organic) spiritual level of development, first personally and then on a culturally expansive plane of growth. Society must stop using the planet as if it were a rubbish dump, and realise that we are ourselves, a part of the organic nature of things, not a race of superior beings reliant upon some omnipotent deity.

Development, healing and true wisdom (of the earth and us) must start on the individual level, not as a herd instinct, like the blind leading the blind. Paganism, in it's earliest unadulterated Shamanistic origins, links man with the manifold forces that ebb and flow through, within and outside him/her self, the forces that cause the river to rise, the Sun to shine, the flowers to bloom, and the birds to fly. First awareness for many individuals of the deep rift betwixt contemporary society and man's place in nature, often materialises as a personal inner conflict. One may have a deep love and affinity for the vitality of trees, sea-shore, mountains and all aspects of nature's bounty, however it may (and will) for many, be marred with a disturbing repulsion of what man has done to this lovely planet.

The present day anti-organic, pro-pollution world view has a great deal to answer for, and more and more individuals are slowly but surely waking up to this 'crystal clear' fact.

We have a state where Governments, industries and companies worldwide, treat the fragile natural environment as if it were a dispensable garbage tip to be fully used and abused as they see fit, and to 'hell' with the future ramifications. We have sadly observed the drastic effect that the historical missionary mind-set has instilled on indigenous cultures like the North American Indian, Australian Aborigine, Eskimo, Amazon Indian etc. The offer of a supposedly superior religious way of life has destroyed many native cultures, eventually leading to the peoples of these ancient misunderstood socio/religious structures losing their original birthright and wisdoms for the dubious honour of a ramshackle wooden church, and the chance to be 'enlightened' by the new white-faced invaders from a strange far off land. Enlightenment that would cost the native peoples, virtually everything they once held dear. The old maxim 'beware of strangers bearing gifts' never rang so true.

The religious crusaders could, if they only had eyes and ears to see and hear, have learnt great knowledge and wisdoms from these peoples, wisdoms that the white-faced ones once long ago also possessed, but had now forgotten. All ancient Pagan religious belief systems, offer modern man the chance to tap into the very essence of life itself, primarily because they, unlike contemporary man-made faiths actually relate to our place in the natural environment. Paganism both old and new, places individual responsibility high on the list of spiritual priorities.

Pagans did not (and do not) worship nature, as is often quoted by others. Pagans link intimately with their Gods/Goddesses, as a way of attuning themselves to the manifold energies present in (and behind) nature, including themselves. All the old pantheons are equally valid; Norse Celtic, Greek, Saxon, African, Egyptian etc, all hold the keys needed to discover one's inner self, future destiny and inherent Pagan birth right. For modern Pagans, working with any particular grouping of Godforms is a personal, exciting and very intimate process, that leads to increased spiritual maturity and awareness. Much confusion has in the past been levelled at the Pagan concept of worshipping/ revering many various Gods/ Goddesses. Pagan deities are symbolic of various expressions of the consciousness inherent in human form. They stand firm as mighty bastions of man's deep need to give his multifarious experiences an anchor in life's turbulent sea.

Early man fearfully observed the rudimentary energy forces of fire, earth, air, and water, and gave them an independent, archetypal existence, by correlating them to other forces that were of a similar nature. With his limited use of language and restricted capacity to project complex or profoundly moving experiences, symbolic exaggeration became the order of the day. The terrifying rage of a forest fire threatening both man and beast, would possibly be depicted on a cave wall as a fearsome devouring lion or tiger. A thunderous storm crashing loudly through the night, might take on the symbolic form of a mighty Golden Hawk or Eagle; and the destructive terror of a giant tidal wave, would sometimes be represented as a horrifying serpent God rightly to be feared and respected.

Even without the gift of language, ancient man would have had no problem at all correlating, exchanging, and generally melding his elemental God-form conceptions with other individuals crossing his path, who had experienced similar revelations on this level of human development. Our human reactions to the primordial forces of nature, mystical experience, unconscious wisdoms and paranormal ability, are constant and unchanging.

Conversely modern society, with it's mind altering stress factors, anxiety and blind reliance on technology, does not remain stable. One decade after another sees drastic transformations in our conscious reaction to these fluctuating forces. The ancient God-forms of our ancestors remain the same, the aspects of human consciousness that work through us allowing laughter, love, fear, joy etc, are as valid today as they were many, many thousands of years ago. They are not 'man-made' in the sense of contemporary religious faith, they are an aspect of human response to the forces outside normal comprehension and understanding, they are essentially "cause and effect" in origin. These archetypal symbols are depicted in strikingly similar fashion throughout world culture and time periods.

They are analogous simply because our human interaction with external and internal energy force is uniform and continuous, regardless of creed, race or historical genealogy. The human response to any emotion be it love or fear, is still felt today just as it was in the long distant past by Norsemen, Celt, Roman or Ancient Greek. Thus the perfect embodiments of these vitalised human traits (the Gods) remain unchanging and timeless.

Todays Pagan minorities invoke the old Gods just like their ancestors did before them, through ritual invocation of their chosen God-form. These God-forms are real when approached with a genuine heart, and can lead to the individual

'THE PATHWAY'

PVR. 95.

experiencing increased spiritual, mental and universal awareness of self, and his/her place within the cosmic order of things.

It is impossible to fully describe the total sum benefit, gained by becoming a practitioner of the Old Paths, and personal insight into this aspect of life's wondrously magical side, must really be experienced on the individual level to be appreciated in it's entirety. Contemporary Paganism is a path, or more correctly a series of related spiritual paths traceable back to the very dawn of time. Each individual Pagan will, when asked to describe their religious concepts, give a (thankfully) different answer, this is because unlike strict monotheistic faith, Paganism is not of a rigid doctrinal nature, and that is the way it should always be.

With Paganism, individualism is the name of the game. Every person must follow their own spiritual path, simply because every person is of a unique nature. Some will follow one particular pantheon of deities local to the vicinity where they were born. British or Irish people may choose to attune with Gods/Goddesses like Brigantia, Midir, Nudd or Epona, while some folk feel more at home with more exotic deities like Osiris, Bast, Tammuz or Rhea. Some incorporate many various cross paralleled Gods into their path, others relate to elder faiths that prior to Christianity's monopoly, reached these Isles through Saxon, Norse, Gaulish invasion.

There is in fact a great deal of common sense for modern Pagans to attune themselves to the more indigenous deity patterns, as local God-forms always possess much greater vitality and kinship with the native soil. The term *'indigenous'* can however, be more encapsulating than it may at first seem. All ancient Pagan inroads to a land, no matter how long ago, sooner or later leave their own indelible psychic footprint. The once alien/exotic deities eventually become indigenous to the very place that previously sought to deny them access. There is a great and understandable desire expressed by many neo Pagans in tracing back and relating to the earlier pre-Christian faiths of their given land. However one must guard against a type of dangerous elitism that says, *"my Gods are older or more authentic than yours "*.

Every person has their own special psychological background that has evolved through educational and parental factors as well, moreover earlier personal experiences both good and bad forge one's character to what it is today. This in turn leads one to their own quest for individual spiritual liberation, what is right for one person may be wrong for another, even if the individuals concerned came from seemingly alike origins. Because of this fact, the God-forms used by one person may appear/feel wrong to his/her peers. Such individualism is absolutely vital to the evolution of humanity as a species, and diversity, spiritual or otherwise must be appreciated for the *'Gods'* given blessing that it really is. The level of intellectual capacity, psychological development and state of psychic awareness displayed by the individual directly affects the type of deities that will appeal to his/her spiritual nature and affinity. Active, young people may be drawn to exhilarating deities like Thor, Lugh or Diana, God forms that intimately reflect the vitality felt in youths struggle for self-esteem and maturity.

Those in need of comfort or love will invoke the assistance of Venus, Baldur, Eros etc, while the studious intellectual may call upon Thoth, Minerva or Ogma to help with a complex problem before revision. Each different God-form is a small but vital component of the indispensable evolutionary force inherent in creation, to deny or ignore these essential archetypes is to invite imbalance, paranoia, inhibition and the inexorable disintegration of human development on all levels. When we invoke the old Gods to assist us in our lives, we are in fact synchronising and attuning ourselves to the timeless wonders of creation that developed out of primordial chaos. By intimately harmonising with a given God-form, for instance Venus for love, or Mercury for safe journeys, we become of a single track mentality.

All other outside worldly distractions are put to one side and become irrelevant as we form an awesome bonding with the deity concerned. During this exchange of energy our mundane every day consciousness is momentarily halted, then transcended by the sheer tidal swell of the God force. Following this experience we can (and certainly do) have access to greater levels of cosmic revelation, spiritual perception and magical awareness. Realms of previously untapped knowledge and wisdoms become within our grasp, moreover the energy received from the invocation of the deity provides us with many insights that could not be possibly gained any other way.

The energy exchange with a God-form is a magically beautiful encounter that can only improve us mentally, physically and spiritually. It also leads to a much greater appreciation of all aspects of the wondrous natural cycles of life, including our fellow humans and other living creatures. More and more individuals (including Christians) are beginning to feel a growing sense of despair regarding the spiritual imbalance, hypocrisy, intolerance and disintegration in contemporary society. Absolutist faiths that have a type of superior 'our God reigns' sort of doctrine and mentality, can only lead to eventual destruction, war and misery. Regrettably history proves this as indisputable fact.

A return to the balanced ways of the Earth, our ancient ancestors and the Old Gods is urgently needed, if this culture is to ever drag itself out of the present mindless mess. We have to move forward on an 'individual' level, not as a herd or flock controlled by spiritual leaders with third hand censored information. Understanding the mythological wisdoms of our Pagan pre-Christian faiths, festivals, customs and traditions stands as one vital step to individual contribution towards a more tolerant society. Mankind and the planet cannot wait, time is quickly running out. The ominous escalation of modern weaponry systems, industrial capability to pollute the environment with toxic waste, manic stupidity of officialdoms road-scheme destruction of ancient forest, and modern mans insane desire to totally exploit some species to extinction etc. all bear witness to the ' man is superior to and must suppress the rest of the natural world' state of mind, currently inflicted on society. Anybody doubting this concept should closely examine the early church's dualistic attitude to the worldly realm.

The Earth and all its inhabitants has always been regarded Biblically as dwelling in *'Satan's kingdom'*, while God's place was the higher spiritual place of Heaven. This distortion of natural cosmic law has unfortunately left the flood gates open for all manner of human irresponsibilities to the planet. Man's inhumanity to his/her environment is then yet another sad legacy of the dualistic imprinting process. The early monotheistic idea of material earthly things being equated with evil, and spiritual things being connected to goodness, have created much of the universal confusion in today's society. Paganisms crystalline concept of all levels of reality - physical, mental, astral, spiritual etc being interconnected and working in unison, not against one another (as in the black/white dual- istic mind-set) comes as an ancient revelation again revived. The material level of existence is not intrinsically evil, it is just as essential as all other planes of reality, moreover it is the concrete manifestation of what starts on higher bastions of existence.

The Pagan revival is slowly but surely gaining momentum, it will not happen overnight (Rome wasn't built in a day). Monotheistic cults like Christianity may seem quite old, however compared to the awesome timespan previously held by earlier Heathen faiths, they are a mere drop in the ocean of human spirituality. Man made religions come and go, some last a bit longer than others before they go in the way of the dinosaur - extinct ! Alternatively Paganism may be perceived as like the young God Adonis, awakening from it's 2000 year old repose, to again take up it's formally lost position in the field of human spiritual growth. The Gods created us, and we in turn give them solid materialisation through our conscious awareness of self, and the complex but beautiful ways of the hills, trees, river and sea.

Monotheistic hierarchies of the day will protest, rebel and generally invoke damnation, however the human spirit shall eventually shine through the darkness of theological suppression. Balance must be restored before it is too late for humanity and this fragile planet of ours. Like bursting shoots in May, the Old Gods cannot wait any longer.

Useful Addresses

British Druid Order, P O Box 29, St Leonards on Sea, East Sussex, TN37 7YP

OBOD (Order of Bards Ovates & Druids), P O Box 1333, Lewes, East Sussex, BN7 3ZG

Pagan Anti-Defamation League, 286 Guildford Road, Southport, Merseyside, PR8 3EB

The Pagan Federation, BM Box 7097, London, WC1N 3XX

When contacting these groups, please enclose an SAE. or International Reply Coupon.

Index

FREE DETAILED CATALOGUE

A detailed illustrated catalogue is available on request, SAE or International Postal Coupon appreciated. Titles are available direct from Capall Bann, post free in the UK (cheque or PO with order) or from good bookshops and specialist outlets. Title currently available include:

Animals, Mind Body Spirit & Folklore
Angels and Goddesses - Celtic Christianity & Paganism by Michael Howard
Arthur - The Legend Unveiled by C Johnson & E Lung
Auguries and Omens - The Magical Lore of Birds by Yvonne Aburrow
Book of the Veil The by Peter Paddon
Call of the Horned Piper by Nigel Jackson
Cats' Company by Ann Walker
Celtic Lore & Druidic Ritual by Rhiannon Ryall
Compleat Vampyre - The Vampyre Shaman: Werewolves & Witchery by Nigel Jackson
Crystal Clear - A Guide to Quartz Crystal by Jennifer Dent
Earth Dance - A Year of Pagan Rituals by Jan Brodie

Earth Magic by Margaret McArthur
Enchanted Forest - The Magical Lore of Trees by Yvonne Aburrow
Healing Homes by Jennifer Dent
Herbcraft - Shamanic & Ritual Use of Herbs by Susan Lavender & Anna Franklin
In Search of Herne the Hunter by Eric Fitch
Inner Space Workbook - Developing Counselling & Magical Skills Through the Tarot
Kecks, Keddles & Kesh by Michael Bayley
Living Tarot by Ann Walker
Magical Incenses and Perfumes by Jan Brodie
Magical Lore of Animals by Yvonne Aburrow
Magical Lore of Cats by Marion Davies

Magical Lore of Herbs by Marion Davies
Masks of Misrule - The Horned God & His Cult in Europe by Nigel Jackson
Mysteries of the Runes by Michael Howard
Oracle of Geomancy by Nigel Pennick
Patchwork of Magic by Julia Day
Pathworking - A Practical Book of Guided Meditations by Pete Jennings
Pickingill Papers - The Origins of Gardnerian Wicca by Michael Howard
Psychic Animals by Dennis Bardens
Psychic Self Defence - Real Solutions by Jan Brodie
Runic Astrology by Nigel Pennick
Sacred Grove - The Mysteries of the Forest by Yvonne Aburrow
Sacred Geometry by Nigel Pennick
Sacred Lore of Horses The by Marion Davies
Sacred Ring - Pagan Origins British Folk Festivals & Customs by Michael Howard
Secret Places of the Goddess by Philip Heselton
Talking to the Earth by Gordon Maclellan
Taming the Wolf - Full Moon Meditations by Steve Hounsome
The Goddess Year by Nigel Pennick & Helen Field
West Country Wicca by Rhiannon Ryall
Witches of Oz The by Matthew & Julia Phillips

Capall Bann is owned and run by people actively involved in many of the areas in which we publish. Our list is expanding rapidly so do contact us for details on the latest releases. We guarantee our mailing list will never be released to other companies or organisations.

Capall Bann Publishing, Freshfields, Chieveley, Berks, RG20 8TF.